Distributed School Leadership

Tomorrow's schools will need new forms of leadership. The old hierarchical models of leadership simply do not fit any longer. We need to develop new leaders at all levels of the system if we are serious about sustaining improvement and change. But how do we go about this?

This book focuses on the *why*, *how* and *what* of distributed leadership by offering a practical insight into what it looks like in schools. It argues that our new system leaders are already in schools and that the main challenge is to develop them and maximise their collective capacity to make a difference. Drawing on the 'Developing Leaders Programme', which aims to develop young leaders in schools, it provides practical examples and case-study evidence of distributed leadership in action. The main aims of the book are to:

- provide a clear account of distributed leadership in schools
- offer evidence about its positive impact on organisational and individual learning
- give case-study exemplars and practical illustrations of how distributed leadership works in practice.

The book also considers the leadership of networks and the federations. It looks at how lateral capacity is built and the part distributed leadership plays in generating leadership capacity within and between schools. It will be of interest to head teachers, aspiring school leaders, teachers and educational professionals.

Alma Harris is Professor of Educational Leadership at the London Centre for Leadership in Learning, Institute of Education, University of London, UK. She is also Associate Director of the Specialist Schools and Academies Trust.

Leading School Transformation Series

Series Editors:

Alma Harris
University of London, UK

Claire Mathews
Head of Leadership programmes, Specialist Schools and Academies Trust

Sue Williamson
Director of Leadership and Innovation, Specialist Schools and Academies Trust

The Leading School Transformation series brings together leading researchers and writers to identify the latest thinking about new and innovative leadership practices that transform schools and school systems. The books have been written with educational professionals in mind, and draw upon the latest international research and evidence to offer new ways of thinking about leadership, provide examples of leadership in practice and identify concrete ways of transforming leadership for schools and school systems in the future.

Titles in the series

Raising the Stakes
From improvement to transformation in the reform of schools
Brian J. Caldwell and Jim M. Spinks

Leadership Mindsets
Innovation and learning in the transformation of schools
Linda Kaser and Judy Halbert

Distributed School Leadership

Developing tomorrow's leaders

Alma Harris

 **Routledge**
Taylor & Francis Group

LONDON AND NEW YORK

 Specialist Schools
and Academies Trust
EXCELLENCE AND DIVERSITY

First published 2008
by Routledge
2 Park Square, Milton Park, Abingdon, Oxon OX14 4RN, UK

Simultaneously published in the USA and Canada
by Routledge
270 Madison Ave, New York, NY 10016

Routledge is an imprint of the Taylor & Francis Group, an informa business

© 2008 Alma Harris

Reprinted 2008

Typeset in Garamond3 by
RefineCatch Limited, Bungay, Suffolk
Printed and bound in Great Britain by
Cpod, Trowbridge, Wiltshire

British Library Cataloguing in Publication Data
A catalogue record for this book is available from the British Library

Library of Congress Cataloging in Publication Data
Harris, Alma, 1958–
Distributed school leadership : developing tomorrow's leaders /
Alma Harris.
p. cm.
1. Educational leadership.   2. School improvement programs.
3. Educational equalization.   I. Title.
LB2831.6.H37 2008
371.2'07—dc22   2008003331

ISBN10: 0–415–41957–3 (hbk)
ISBN10: 0–415–41958–1 (pbk)

ISBN13: 978–0–415–41957–4 (hbk)
ISBN13: 978–0–415–41958–1 (pbk)

April 21, 2009

For Claire

Contents

Illustrations

Acknowledgement

I am very grateful to the head teachers and staff of all the case study schools who gave their time so generously. I also acknowledge the Specialist Schools and Academies Trust (SSAT) and the National College for School Leadership (NCSL) who funded the research projects that provided some of the data about distributed leadership practices.

I am particularly grateful to David Crossley, Tom Clarke and Janet Aldridge for allowing me to draw upon the cases in the 'Beyond Workforce Reform' Project, and to Emma Sims of the SSAT and Gillian Ireson of the NCSL for allowing me to draw on the 'Deep Leadership' work. I also acknowledge Professor Andy Hargreaves and the 'Beyond Expectations' project team.

Thanks to Dean Fink for providing such valuable feedback on the penultimate draft and to Jim Spillane for his friendship and intellectual contribution.

Finally, I am grateful to Anna Clarkson and Lucy Wainwright of Routledge for their support for the iNET/SSAT leadership series, and to my co-editors Sue Williamson and Clare Mathews.

Foreword

Fads are commonplace in education, especially in school leadership and management. Moreover, faddism is as common in the halls of academia as in the schoolhouse. In an effort to be seen to be doing something new, scholars, policymakers, and practitioners don the latest fashion. Efforts over the past decade or so to articulate and develop a distributed perspective on school leadership and management are certainly in vogue but may turn out as just another educational fad, adopted by school leadership scholars and practitioners but soon discarded. Time will tell. In the meantime, books such as this one that engage the field in a critical dialogue about what it means to take a distributed perspective are the best methods we have of stop the tide of faddism.

Theoretically anchored, Harris takes a functional or pragmatic approach to distributed leadership. Looking at what distributed leadership looks like on the ground in real schools, she examines with concrete examples how a distributed perspective on leadership might make a difference for learning at both the individual and organisational levels. With rich examples from the trenches, the pages that follow bring alive for the reader the entailments in practice of taking a distributed perspective to leadership and management. These views from the field not only offer glimpses of what is, but are also evocative of what might be.

Attending to the broader socio-political context of shifting policy environments, changing demographics, and an education apartheid that increasingly separates the rich from the poor in terms of access to knowledge, the book makes a convincing case for the need for attention to school leadership and management. Tying these broader environmental shifts with the ever challenging and more demanding job of formally designated leaders, the book offers a convincing case for serious attention to school leadership and its improvement. Moreover, Harris argues convincingly that new tools are needed to undertake that work. The various chapters not only make the case for these tools, but also sketch some of their features and offer examples of what they might look like on the ground in real schools.

Combing numerous literatures both within the field of education and outside it, the book offers some fresh ideas on a familiar phenomenon – school leadership and management. Connecting work on distributed leadership to scholarship on organisational learning and knowledge creation, the book points to the heart of school improvement – knowledge, creation and diffusion in schools and school systems. The chapters offer helpful pointers as to how those interested in improving school leadership might begin to think about how the structure of schools, both actual and imagined structures, might enable and constrain knowledge production and dissemination.

The attempt to imagine schools for the future is provocative. Of course, time will be the judge of the durability of these ideas about how schools might be reorganised. Imagining brave new worlds is considerably easier than putting them into practice. But it is a critical first step.

Jim Spillane
Chicago, USA
December 2007

Chapter 1

Leadership in a changing world

> As models of leadership shift from the organisational hierarchies with leaders at the top to more distributed, shared networks, people will need to be deeply committed to cultivating their capacity to serve what's seeking to emerge
>
> (Senge et al, 2005:186)

> Within each of the developed countries, including the United States, average life expectancy is five, ten or even fifteen years shorter for people living in the poorest areas compared to those living in the richest
>
> (Wilkinson, 2005:1).

In today's climate of rapid change and increasingly high expectations, effective leadership is needed more than ever. But the question is what type of leadership? It is clear that change on such a massive scale will demand new leadership practices but the precise forms of leadership required to grapple with the complexities and challenges of technological advancement and globalisation remain unclear. The increasing integration of world economies through trade and financial transactions has created emerging market economies that are more integrated and interdependent (Zhao, 2007). Economic globalisation has outpaced the globalisation of politics and mindsets (Stiglitz, 2006:25). The traditional economic boundaries between countries are rapidly becoming less and less relevant. The global economy is booming.

But globalisation has also become a crisis in many parts of the world (Zhao, 2007:18). Despite increasing levels of wealth and prosperity around the globe, relative levels of poverty are higher than ever before and the gaps between rich and poor are widening. As the economic market place of the world is changing, in both developed and less developed countries, there is an increasing disparity between those who have high quality education and those who do not.

Although the wealth of the most affluent nations has soared, there is a growing underclass of citizens living in poverty. In her book *The Shock Doctrine*, Naomi Klein (2007) asserts that poverty, misery and human suffering are a necessary part of new 'disaster' capitalism. She challenges how far the global free market has triumphed democratically and argues that America's 'free market' policies have come to dominate the world – through the exploitation of disaster-shocked people and countries.

In his analysis of the relationship between poverty and educational attainment, David Berliner (2005) highlights the fact that the United States has the highest rate among industrialised countries of those that are permanently poor. As the Figure 1.1 below shows, only Mexico has a higher rate with the UK in fourth position with 19.8 per cent.

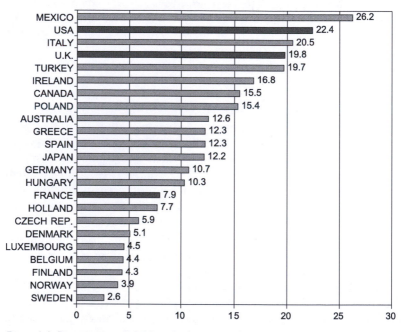

Figure 1.1 **Percentage of children living in 'relative' poverty defined as households with income below 50 per cent of the national median income (UNICEF, 1999, http://www.unicef.org/).**

Berliner (2005) also points out that many of the wealthy countries, like the USA and the UK, have few mechanisms to get people out of poverty once they fall into it. So those who become impoverished through illness, divorce, or job loss are likely to remain poor.

While the rich have become richer, the poor have become poorer. Those who are well educated have access to the richest economic system the world has ever known. For those who lack education, the door of opportunity is 'slammed shut' (Barr and Parrett, 2007:7). As Berliner (2005:15) argues, 'poverty restricts the expression of generic talent at the lower end of the socio-economic scale'. It is clear that poverty limits life chances as well as educational achievement.

The moral imperative to address issues of poverty is clear, so is the educational imperative. The gap between the educational attainment of the poorest and the most affluent students is getting larger, even though overall levels of performance may have increased. As Fullan (2006:7) argues, we urgently need to 'raise the economic bar and close the gap between the richest and the poorest'. Clearly no one would disagree. But what kind of education will be required to close the gap, what kind of schools, what kind of leadership?

This book is primarily concerned with addressing the educational apartheid that separates the rich from the poor so starkly in terms of educational attainment. The book focuses particularly on school leadership as *one* means of improving learning for *all students in all school settings*. It argues that leadership is a powerful and important force for change in schools and school systems.

As the McKinsey (2007:71) report noted:

> School reforms rarely succeed without effective leadership both at the level of the system and at the level of the individual schools. There is not a single documented case of a school successfully turning around its pupil achievement trajectory in the absence of talented leadership. Similarly we did not find a single school system which had been turned around that did not possess sustained, committed and talented leadership.

The main challenge facing schools and school systems is how to locate, develop and sustain committed and talented leadership. How do we find the *leaders of tomorrow* and keep them in our schools and school systems? How do we nurture, grow and develop broad-based leadership capacity in our schools?

This book suggests that to identify and develop the *leaders of tomorrow* is both urgent and necessary for system transformation. It suggests that to release the leadership capability and capacity in our schools we need to alter structures, redefine boundaries and remove barriers that prevent broad-based involvement of the many rather than the few in leadership. But it is more than just about changing structures. The most effective schools and school systems invest in *developing leaders.* They actively seek out leadership talent,[1] and provide development opportunities for those in the very early stages of their career (Harris and Townsend, 2007).

In 2007 Finland was at the top of educational performance tables. Teaching in Finland is a high status profession with ten applicants for every teacher-training place. All school leaders teach and also take on a system-wide responsibility, supporting change and development in other schools. Within Finland, schooling is viewed as a public and not a private good and the school system is based upon the core values of trust, co-operation and responsibility.

In contrast the US and English school systems are based on high accountability mechanisms and low trust of teachers. Leaders in many schools are far too busy to teach, even if they wanted to. So how do we re-organise schools and school systems so that leaders are closer to learning? How do we re-engage with the moral purpose of education and produce *tomorrow's leaders* who put learning before targets?

Closing the attainment gap will not be secured simply by providing more school leaders. This will only be achieved by ameliorating the negative and pervasive social and economic conditions that influence communities and the life chances of young people. Any attempts at educational improvement can only be part, and possibly only a small part, of the wider agenda of reducing social and economic inequalities in society (West and Pennell, 2003; Harris and Ranson, 2005).

We know that within school factors or influences cannot offset the forces of deprivation. However it is clear that schools *can make* a difference and *do make* a difference to the life chances of young people, particularly those young people in the poorest communities (Harris et al, 2006a, 2006b; Reynolds et al, 2006). Within all schools but particularly high-poverty schools, leadership is a critical component in reversing low expectations and low performance. The quality of leadership has been shown to be the most powerful

1 See 'Developing Leaders' Programme: www.ssat.org.uk.

influence on learning outcomes, second only to curriculum and instruction (Leithwood et al, 2006a, 2006b). The question is what type or form of school leadership is most likely to secure learning success for all children in all contexts?

This book takes a long, hard look at distributed leadership as one emerging form of leadership practice in schools. It examines distributed leadership from the perspective of theory, practice and empirical evidence. It explores whether distributed leadership has the potential to improve learning at the organisation and individual level. As Youngs (2007:1) has pointed out, 'issues of popularisation mean that distributed forms of leadership may end up being yet another "fad" '. This is certainly true. It is important therefore to stand back and take a critical, informed and empirically based look at distributed leadership.

If distributed leadership is found to be little more than delegation, then we need to know that and move on. If it has the potential to broaden our understanding of school leadership and allows us to suspend and possibly relinquish our conventional and dominant views of leadership, it is worth pursuing. As Youngs (2007:1) points out, the latter *will require courage*. Distributing leadership within and across school and school systems requires a shift in power and resources. It demands alternative school structures that support alternative forms of leadership. Inevitably, this will generate some criticism, resistance and even derision from those with a vested interest in keeping things just the way they are.

But the pressure for change in school and school systems is now acute. There are many global, national and local trends that will necessitate significant changes in schools and schooling. Globalisation, changing employment opportunities and shifts in the pattern of recruitment of school leaders are powerful forces for change. They cannot be ignored. The pressure for change is relentless and unremitting.

As each of these forces for change is explored in the sections and chapters that follow, it is important to remember that the prime reason for thinking about alternative ways of organising schools and adopting different approaches to leadership is to make the learning experiences of *all* young people better. It is primarily concerned with the educational success of every student, irrespective of background or context.

The analysis of social, economic and global 'change forces' suggests that we urgently need new organisational forms and leadership practices within our schools and school systems. We cannot have twentieth century structures shaping twenty-first century leadership practices. But none of these change forces is as important as the moral purpose of education. Put simply, if we are committed to changing leadership structures and practices in our schools, we do it because we believe it will improve the learning and life chances of all our students.

Globalisation

As a force for change, globalisation is rapidly reshaping societies and cultures on a massive scale. Work is being redefined and organisational boundaries are being redrawn. The pace of change is relentless, even frantic, and the demands for improvements in schooling unprecedented. As Bernake (2006:833) points out, 'rather than producing goods in a single process in a single location, firms are increasingly breaking the production process into discrete steps and performing each step in whatever location allows them to minimise costs'. Theoretically, a business can employ anyone, at any time, anywhere in the world. Outsourcing is now commonplace and millions of Chinese and Indians are working for US businesses located in any of the three countries (Zhao, 2007:832). The global market place is fast, complex and diverse.

Thomas Friedman (2006) talks about ten forces that have re-defined and re-shaped the 'flat world' in the twenty-first century (Friedman, 2006:828). His basic argument is that the boundaries and barriers to global business have largely disappeared creating a flatter world and a more competitive environment. He points out that the type of leadership required in the 'flat world' is one that embodies *creativity, flexibility, portability and ingenuity*. It is a form of leadership that cannot be restricted by structures or organisational boundaries.

Despite such powerful global trends, leadership is still thought about in a rather traditional way. As Senge et al (2005) propose:

> One of the road blocks for groups moving forward now is thinking that they have to wait for a leader to emerge – someone who embodies the future path. I think the key to going forward is nurturing a new form of leadership that does not depend on extraordinary individuals. (p 185)

Across all organisations the future competitive edge will be the *creative* edge. In all sectors, the premier organisations will be singled out by their ability to be transformative and innovative. Leadership will be required that will secure transformation and rapid change. Lightning-swift advances in technology and communication will undoubtedly create greater challenges for leaders and leadership. This is particularly true of schools.

As the link between individuals and their organisations is weakening, patterns of activity are shifting away from a central location and point of control. As organisational functioning becomes more geographically dispersed, it remains questionable whether existing leadership practice, particularly its hierarchical form, can survive. Senge et al (2005) suggest that 'in a world of global networks we face issues for which hierarchical leadership is inherently inadequate' (p 186). Their work suggests that as long as our thinking is governed by concepts from the 'machine age' we will continue to recreate institutions as they were in the past, and leadership practices suited for institutions belonging to another era.

Seeing leadership in a different way requires stopping our habitual ways of thinking about leadership and leadership practice. The capacity to suspend established ways of seeing is essential for all-important scientific discoveries. It requires what Senge et al (2005:84) term 'sensing an emerging future', where old frameworks are not imposed on new realities. As the pace of technological development quickens, so does the rate of what Joseph Schumpeter (1942) has called the 'creative destruction' – of products, companies and even entire industries. Little is predictable or repetitive, and 'overall businesses operate less and less like halls of production and more and more like a kind of casino of knowledge' (Senge et al, 2005:84).

In his work, David Hargreaves (2007) argues that system leadership requires more than head teachers securing sustainable system-level change. He suggests that *system redesign* is needed to improve the architecture of schooling, and highlights how leadership is a powerful force of reconfiguration in the redesign of the system (Hargreaves, 2007:27). This leadership configuration has five components:

- flatter, less hierarchical staff structure;
- distributed leadership;
- student leadership;
- leadership development and succession;
- participative decision-making processes.

Hargreaves (2007) argues that these five components are already in place in many schools, and that system redesign will emerge as schools drive the process of transformation and change.

The educational environment has shifted so dramatically and so permanently that we need to reconsider what we understand by leadership and leadership practice in schools. In many countries, schools are no longer at the centre of educational provision. Multi-agency working, partnership and networks are the common denominators of contemporary educational change. They are demanding and creating alternative leadership practices. Inter-institutional collaboration and multi-agency working are also providing the platforms for new leaders to emerge. Support staff, parents, students and multi agency professionals are all potential leaders and change agents.

In the 'brave new' economic world, schools will need to harness all the available leadership capacity and capability. This will only be achieved if schools maximise all forms of human, social and intellectual capital. To maximise leadership capacity schools need to be operating and performing at the level of the best schools. To achieve this requires a radical shift in leadership practice.

Good to Great

In the opening line of his book *Good to Great*, Jim Collins (2001) states that 'good is the enemy of great', and argues that one of the reasons why we don't have great schools *is because we have good schools*. The vast majority of our schools, he suggests, never become great because the vast majority become quite good. If we accept this argument and ask what it takes for schools to become 'great schools' rather than good schools, we inevitably come back to leadership.

The research base is fairly unequivocal; leadership is an important lever in organisational change and development (Leithwood et al, 2006a, 2006b). It is a powerful mechanism for school improvement and is a major force for organisational transformation (Fullan, 2006: Fullan et al, 2007). Evidence suggests that school leadership influences student learning outcomes and that the impact of leadership upon student learning *is significant* (Leithwood et al, 2006a, 2006b).

Jim Collins and his researchers found, largely as they expected, that leadership was a key factor in the success of the 'good to great' companies. However, the researchers were surprised with their findings about the type of leadership in 'good to great' companies. Instead of the autocratic or charismatic leader they found leaders who were modest, determined, humble but fearless. The researchers found that the most effective leaders invested in the leadership of others and in building leadership capacity for even greater success in the next generation.

Leadership was graded at five levels and at the top level (level 5) the leaders actively distributed leadership and purposefully and deliberately built strong, self-sufficient teams. The 'good to great' leaders generated and supported multi-level leadership in order to build the commitment and consensus for continual transformation. The research also found, somewhat controversially, that charismatic leadership could be a liability as much as an asset. Often it deterred people from bringing leaders the 'brutal facts' required for meaningful change to take place (Collins, 2001:89).

There is growing evidence to suggest that distributed forms of leadership can positively influence organisational development and change (Harris et al, 2007; Leithwood et al, 2007). The evidence base about distributed leadership and organisational change, although still emerging, is encouraging. It tends to suggest that 'school leadership has a greater influence on schools and students when it is widely distributed' (Leithwood et al, 2006a, 2006b; 2007). This position inevitably challenges the traditional notion of the singular leader and implies broad-based involvement in the practice of leadership in schools.

In his work, Caldwell (2006) talks about the 'new image of the self-managing school' as one where the student is the most important unit of the organisation, not the classroom or the school. He argues that schools cannot achieve transformation by acting *alone* or operating in a line of support from the centre of the school system, to the school, to the department to the classroom. The success of the school, he suggests, depends upon its 'capacity to join networks or federations to share knowledge, address problems and pool resources' (Caldwell, 2006:75). This capacity, he suggests, requires leadership that is distributed across schools in networks and federations as well as within schools across programmes of teaching and learning.

The education terrain is shifting and the existing structures and boundaries of schooling are fast eroding. Education is being revolutionised through the Internet, GOOGLE, outsourcing and the demands and expectations of a 24/7 generation. Those organisations destined to be 'great' in the rapidly transforming world will be those adept at generating new leadership capacity to meet the changing demands of global schooling.

Hargreaves and Fink (2006:95) argue that 'sustainable leadership is leadership that spreads, that is distributed and shared'. They suggest that 'sustainable and distributed leadership inspires staff members, students and parents to seek, create and exploit leadership opportunities that contribute to deep and broad learning for students' (p 95). In short, distributed leadership implies broad-based involvement in leadership practice (Harris and Lambert, 2003). It also requires restructuring and risk taking by those in formal leadership positions. It requires rearranging and removing those structural barriers that prevent teachers and other professionals working together most effectively.

Fitzgerald and Gunter (2007) question whether it is possible for teacher leadership or distributed leadership practices to occur in 'a policy climate that affords authority and responsibility for leadership and management to those labelled according to an established hierarchy'. The implication here is that existing structures mediate against distributed leadership practice and that this type of informal influence and agency is not possible within the existing hierarchical structure of schooling.

The research evidence shows that distributed leadership occurs in even the most hierarchically configured and tightly structured organisation (Day et al, 2007). Clearly, some patterns of distribution are less possible within certain organisational constraints, but it is not the case that distributed leadership or teacher leadership cannot occur within the *established hierarchy* (Fitzgerald and Gunter 2007). The key point here is that leadership, like culture, inevitably permeates the organisation.

Many schools are deliberately changing their structures and working practices in order to distribute leadership more widely and to locate leadership closer to learning and teaching. In England, the workforce remodelling agenda and 'Every Child Matters' have provided schools with a major opportunity to redesign leadership structures and practices. New teams have been constructed, new governance processes implemented, alternative structures assembled and new relationships formulated between schools and other agencies (Harris et al, 2007). The *established hierarchy* of leadership in schools may not have vanished completely but it is fast eroding.

Fitzgerald and Gunter (2007) also suggest that distributed forms of leadership merely cement authority and hierarchy whereby leaders 'monitor teachers and their work to ensure a set of pre-determined standards are met'. It is perfectly possible to see distributed leadership this way. But this view is premised on a particular interpretation of distributed leadership, which sees it as the distribution of 'additional' tasks or demands by others upon teachers. This interpretation equates more with delegation that distribution. It is what Youngs (2007:7) has termed *distributed pain* where the delegating of leadership is a by-product of work intensification.

The teacher leadership literature challenges the notion that distributed leadership is simply delegation by another name. This extensive research base reinforces that teachers actively choose to undertake informal or non-permanent leadership roles in school (Lieberman, 2007). It is not imposed upon them; they choose to take on certain leadership activities, and in many cases instigate the opportunities to lead. The research base also shows that teachers' prime concern in undertaking any leadership role is to improve student learning (Murphy et al, 2006). Teacher leaders are essentially instructional leaders first and foremost.

The evidence also highlights the fact that teachers who lead innovation and change do not necessarily see their role as one of a 'leader'. They operate with a high degree of professional choice, autonomy and responsibility. There is little evidence of coercion into leadership roles, wilful delegation or distribution of unwanted extra tasks. The opportunities provided to innovate at the classroom and school level are not generally construed by teachers as a subtle form of exploitation (Lieberman, 2007).

Clearly much depends on context and intention. Certainly in some schools distribution may equate with delegation. Much depends upon the motivations of those in formal leadership positions and the way they understand distributed leadership. The evidence shows that schools with broad-based distributed leadership tend to have cultures where there is a high degree of professional trust and where relationships between staff are positive.

In their work, Bryk and Schneider (2007) highlight the importance of organisational trust to organisational stability and growth. Their work underlines the importance of high trust and a cohesive culture for distributed leadership to flourish. In her account of competition between leaders in a school, Storey (2004) reveals the frailty of distributed forms of leadership once boundaries and roles overlap. Where individuals did not trust each other and power struggles emerged, distributed leadership breaks down irrecoverably.

Distributed leadership

The purpose of this book is not to publicise or romanticise distributed leadership. To do so would be to fall into the trap of so many, now redundant, theories of leadership that have been promoted without adequate scrutiny or detailed consideration. Instead, the book aims to explore distributed leadership from a number of different perspectives, drawing extensively upon evidence and looking closely at the theory and the practice. The book aims to exemplify and illuminate current and emerging leadership practices in schools from recent work with schools in England. It will also review the evidence base concerning the relationship between distributed forms of leadership and organisational change (Leithwood et al, 2006a, 2006b; Silins and Mulford, 2002; Spillane et al, 2003; Harris and Muijs, 2004).

The book takes a distributed perspective on leadership, not to undermine the role of the head or principal but to explore *how* leadership is distributed and *whether* different patterns of distribution positively or negatively affect organisational outcomes. It is not proposing the removal of all formal leadership structures or processes but rather advocating leadership as the co-performance and interaction of individuals both in formal and informal leadership positions (Spillane and Camburn, 2006).

The book takes an interpretive and normative stance on distributed leadership rather than an *analytical* position. It acknowledges the centrality and major contribution of distributed leadership theory to the field, particularly the contribution of Jim Spillane and his colleagues (Spillane et al, 2001, 2003; Spillane, 2006). This book deliberately moves away from analysis, and chooses to take a *functional or practical* perspective on distributed leadership. The book's main aim is to outline what distributed leadership looks like in schools, and to explore whether it makes a positive difference to learning, both organisational and individual.

A distributed leadership perspective recognises that there are multiple leaders (Spillane and Zoltners Sherer, 2004; 2007) and that leadership activities are widely shared within and between organisations (Harris, 2007a). A distributed model of leadership focuses upon the interactions, rather than the actions, of those in formal and informal leadership roles. It is primarily concerned with *leadership practice* and how leadership influences organisational and instructional improvement (Spillane, 2006). A distributed perspective on leadership acknowledges the work of all individuals who contribute to leadership practice, whether or not they are formally designated or defined as leaders. Distributed leadership is also central to system reconfiguration and organisational redesign, which necessitate lateral, flatter decision making processes (Hargreaves, 2007).

Why the interest?

Distributed leadership is undoubtedly the leadership idea of the moment. It is currently in vogue but why the interest? It has entered the discourse of schooling at a rapid pace and is in danger of being written off because of its popularity as yet another 'leadership fad' (Youngs, 2007). Stepping back, there would appear to be three main reasons for the current popularity of distributed leadership. Firstly, distributed leadership has _empirical power_. There is increasing research evidence (see Chapter 4) that distributed leadership makes a positive difference to organisational outcomes and student learning. While the evidence base is still relatively new, the emerging findings about its relationship to positive organisational change are consistent and encouraging.

There are an increasing number of studies that highlight a powerful relationship between distributed forms of leadership and positive organisational change (Harris et al, 2007). Most recently research has shown that the patterns of leadership distribution matter within an organisation and that distributed leadership practice is more likely to equate with improved organisational performance and outcomes (Leithwood et al, 2004; 2007).

Secondly, distributed leadership has _representational power_. It represents the alternative approaches to leadership that have emerged because of increased external demands and pressures on heads and principals. In England, schools have restructured their leadership teams and created new roles to meet the needs of work force remodelling, 'Every Child Matters' and the extended schools agenda. This re-structuring has allowed distributed and shared leadership practices to be trialled and extended. It is clear that as schools engage with complex collaborative arrangements, distributed forms of leadership will be required to 'cross multiple types of boundaries and to share ideas and insights' (Wenger et al, 2000:123).

In the increasingly complex world of education, more diverse types of leadership will be required that are flexible enough to meet changing challenges and new demands. There is a growing recognition that the old organisational structures of schooling simply do not fit the requirements of learning in the twenty-first century. New models of schooling are emerging based on collaboration, networking and multi-agency working (federations, partnerships, networked learning communities, extended schools, etc). These new and more complex forms of schooling will undoubtedly require more distributed forms of leadership to function effectively.

The third reason for such interest in distributed leadership is because it has *normative power*; it reflects current changes in leadership practice in schools. The growth of what Gronn (2003) has termed *greedy work* in schools has resulted in the expansion of leadership tasks and responsibilities. Heads and principals can no longer be responsible for all the areas requiring leadership in schools. Consequently alternative leadership structures and practices are fast emerging.

The three reasons for the popularity of distributed leadership, although very different, have become blurred resulting in some conceptual confusion in the field (Harris, 2007b). To clarify the concept of distributed leadership requires separating out the analytical, the empirical and the practical, as these are very different lenses and perspectives. If distributed leadership is more than delegating leadership to others, it needs to be conceptually linked to theory, grounded in empirical verification and located in practice.

This book aims to make these links and to offer an in-depth account of *distributed leadership practice*. No doubt, this will bring the response that there are issues of power, authority, legitimacy and micro-politics that are neatly factored out of the analysis. This is true. The book concentrates firstly, on what distributed leadership looks like in schools and secondly, the difference, if any, it makes to learning. It chooses not to spend countless pages deconstructing distributed leadership or overcomplicating the concept.

In a very practical sense we are facing a crisis in leadership in our schools and school systems. While others are debating the intellectual limitations of distributed leadership, time is running out to find alternative forms of leadership practice that can move schools and learning forward. There is a shortage of heads and principals in our schools, so the existing leadership provision is under some threat.

Distributed leadership is the neat solution, surely? Simply divide out the job of the head or principal to others in the organisation and distributed leadership will save the day. This is once again to fall into the trap of equating distribution with delegation. As the next chapter illustrates, we do need to pay attention to the leadership crisis in our schools. But we need to think about leadership practice differently if we are to address the issue of educational transformation in the long term.

Chapter 2

Leadership in crisis

> A culture of distributive leadership that grooms new leaders for
> the next phase must be established
>
> (Fullan, 2006:31)

Introduction

Across many countries there is, or soon will be, a shortage of head
teachers and principals. In the USA, a shortage of highly qualified
principal candidates has been reported by school districts across the
nation. In some parts of the country 60 per cent of principals will
retire, resign or otherwise leave their positions during the next five
years (Peterson, 2002:815).

In England, the story is similar. Over 59 per cent of full-time
heads in the maintained sector in England are aged 50 or over and
the numbers of retirements is forecast to peak to almost 3,500 in
2009 (NCSL, 2006). In addition, there would seem to be a general
reluctance and resistance from those in other formal leadership positions in schools to take on this pivotal role – possibly because they
are best placed to see the extent of the challenges and demands of
headship.

A number of reports outline reasons for the leadership crisis. In
the USA, two factors are seen as being at the core of the problem.
Firstly, school districts are struggling to attract and retain an
adequate supply of highly qualified candidates for leadership roles,
and secondly, principal candidates and existing principals are often
ill-prepared and inadequately supported to manage the demands of
the role (Levine, 2005:818).

In England, an 'Independent Study of School Leadership' has

revealed that many school leaders are struggling to meet all of the demands placed on them (DfES, 2007). It shows that many heads are having difficulty creating the time to engage effectively with the range of areas of responsibility. Part of this pressurised time is due to the sheer volume of operational issues that school leaders now need to address, along with the increasing pressures to meet targets and raise performance. The report also noted that many school leaders felt more comfortable with an operational rather than a strategic role and wanted to spend more time in classrooms (DfES, 2007:6).

While there is widespread recognition of the importance of the involvement of school leaders in teaching and learning processes, the reality is that many heads are becoming more and more disengaged from classroom practice in their schools because of the weight of other demands. Just over one quarter of primary and secondary heads do not teach at all in timetabled lessons and most of the remainder teach for less than five hours a week. In addition, the demands placed upon them mean that head teachers frequently sacrifice teaching time in order to deal with urgent issues.

The growing body of evidence highlights how *far away from class-room matters* school leaders are becoming, through default rather than design. It suggests that many school leaders are overly involved in maintenance matters to the detriment of strategic imperatives. This 'fire-fighting' approach is a by-product of the sheer volume of tasks and expectations placed upon them. In short, leaders in our schools are spending a disproportionate time managing rather than leading.

Tasks related to accountability are consistently identified by heads as the most time-consuming and draining (DfES, 2007). They are the tasks that take leaders away from the 'chalk-face' and the opportunity cost is high. The word 'initiativitis' is a term used by heads in England to encapsulate their deep-rooted frustration at the steady stream of new policy initiatives imposed on schools. Opinion surveys show that while heads in England are still generally positive about their role, they now face a particularly difficult set of demands: high levels of accountability; individual responsibility for performance and a radical shift towards multi-agency ways of working.

The current context of school leadership is therefore one of over-load, complexity and frustration. Not only has the formal leader's role become more challenging and demanding, but also the external environment is continually pressing for change. The twin expect-ations of ever-higher performance, coupled with the drive for collaboration with other schools, and sectors, is proving difficult to reconcile for many schools.

The 'holy grail' of ever higher targets inevitably drives schools to compete with each other and to seek the competitive advantage wherever and whenever possible. The conveyor belt of change keeps initiatives moving but at a substantial cost to schools. All these initiatives compete for precious time, energy and resources among school staff. It is clear that schools are overwhelmed by the multiple initiatives stemming from multiple sources.

But what difference have such initiatives actually made? The McKinsey (2007) report states that 'despite substantial increases in spending and many well-intentioned reform efforts, performance in a large number of schools systems has barely improved in decades'. The report points out that between 1980 and 2005, public spending per student in the USA increased by 73 per cent after allowing for inflation, however actual student outcomes stayed almost the same.

So if the answer to high performing education systems isn't top-down reform or more money, what is it? The McKinsey (2007) report concludes that the answer lies quite simply in 'better teachers with better instructional practices'. It also points toward the need for strong and effective infrastructures within schools that allow teachers to be the best teachers they can be. Such an infrastructure will not be possible without leaders who firstly, understand the need for it and secondly, are willing to change current practices to achieve it, however painful or difficult that may be.

The changing landscape of schooling in England, and in many other countries, is the strongest signal yet of the need for a very different conceptualisation of leadership practice. The future of school leadership, as it is currently configured, does not look bright. In England, data has shown that 43 per cent of deputies do not wish to move on to headship and 70 per cent of middle leaders say they have no desire to be a head teacher. The reasons cited include the accountability pressures and other external stresses already highlighted. Those in other leadership roles, with the best organisational vantage point don't like what they see.

This problem is evidently more acute in some schools than others. Head teacher vacancies are now almost impossible to fill in certain schools in certain areas. Schools located in areas of high poverty with the range of associated social problems are not usually at the top of the list for those seeking headships. A disproportionate number of head teachers in schools in challenging circumstances are in their first headship post. Evidence shows that a high proportion of these heads leave the school and the profession within the first five years. Many schools in challenging circumstances also have a commensurate high turnover of staff, and are the schools least likely to retain head teachers over time (NCSL, 2006). While we may debate the origins, contributing factors or possible solutions, the fact is we have a leadership crisis in our schools.

Two influences

Two powerful influences are fuelling the current leadership crisis. The first influence is demographic change and fluctuation. The second major influence is accountability (Elmore, 2004). In terms of the first influence, that of demographic change, it was both predictable and predicted. The 'baby boomers' are now reaching late middle age and will retire in large numbers over the next five years. This is a trend that is prevalent across many countries.

In England, the demographic pressures will peak in 2009 and the number of school leader retirements will rise to a peak of 3,500 in this year. This means that 15–20 per cent of school leaders will need to be replaced by 2009. It is predicted that the projected shortfall in numbers coming forward for school leadership posts cannot be absorbed by the system and certain geographical areas will present acute problems, over the next two to three years. A vacuum of leadership expertise and experience in the system; both in the short and long term will undoubtedly have a negative impact on schools unless addressed in some way (NCSL, 2006).

Turning next to accountability, it is clear that in virtually every industrialised democracy the idea of accountability for performance has a firm grip on education policy. As Richard Elmore (2006:3) notes, 'the social, economic and political roots of these policies is worthy of its own analysis, suffice to say these roots run deep and the general direction of these policies is relatively immune to change'.

This accountability drive particularly within the USA, Canada and England has placed acute pressure on those in positions of leadership responsibility in schools and school systems. The constant weighing and measuring of school performance, plus the continual stream of policy changes, has meant that many heads and principals are simply finding the stress of the job too great. In short, many are seeking to leave early or retiring through ill health.

At its core, accountability policy implies *individual* responsibility for school performance (Elmore, 2004). It pays only cursory attention to the social and economic factors that so strongly and pervasively influence performance levels in many school contexts. It is premised on the idea that improvement in standards can be achieved by providing clear analysis of performance and testing, measuring and comparing educational outputs. To be clear, there is nothing inherently wrong with accountability, if used appropriately and well. Without accountability the inherent complacency of 'coasting' schools would not be challenged. Without measures of contextual added value there would be no way of holding schools to account for the relative progress pupils make.

But when over used as a mechanism of control, the effects of external accountability can be counter-productive and even detrimental. Both England and the USA, in particular, have experienced some of the negative effects of accountability. Both countries have introduced substantial high stake testing for schools as a means of combining higher achievement with increased teacher and school accountability. As Hargreaves et al (2007) point out, both England and the USA are dominated by the architecture of accountability and 'soulless standardisation'. They also both appear at the very bottom of the UNICEF league table for 'Children's Well-Being'.[1] Those countries at the top of the list such as the Netherlands and Finland have completely different goals; their prime aim is to develop socially responsible young people rather than meeting externally set and determined targets.

As Warwick Mantell (2007) notes:

> Improving test and exam scores . . . is vital to just about everyone who has influence over what happens in our classrooms. Teachers are reminded, by all those who have power over them, that raising the statistics is vital to everything they do. Teachers are forced not merely to pay attention to results. They live and die by them.

In this climate 'teaching to the test' is widespread and the focus of attention is on raising test scores rather than learning. A disproportionate amount of classroom time is spent preparing young people for the test rather than teaching them how to learn effectively. Hargreaves et al (2007:21) refer to a report that revealed that primary

1   See (http://www.unicef.org).

schools in England devote almost half the lessons between January and May to the preparation for the tests for students aged 11, increasing from nine hours a week in January to 12 hours a week in April.

A 'Primary Review'[2] in England highlighted how the test culture is taking its toll on children in primary schools. It states:

> pupils confirm what teachers believe – that primary education is constrained and to a degree determined by the emphasis on test results. Pupils find themselves under pressure to perform well in national tests. (Ward and Bloom, 2007:14)

The increased pressure upon students and teachers to raise test scores and to demonstrate improved levels of achievement is acute. Inevitably the by-product of such pressure is not only stressed teachers and students but also, at worse, 'manifold strategies for cheating and malpractice' (Hargreaves et al, 2007:26), along with tactical decisions to select certain examination courses. This undoubtedly ensures that better results are achieved for the school but at what cost?

Another by product of the accountability system is the inevitable spotlight placed on 'failing schools', those schools that simply seem to be impervious to improvement (Datnow et al, 2002). Almost every developed country has tried to address the issue of 'failing schools' and many have embraced accountability as the ultimate turnaround solution. But as Fullan (2006) notes, the current 'turnaround' strategies are too little too late. They work on only a small part of the problem and unwittingly establish conditions that actually guarantee unsustainability' (p 20). He argues that while tight accountability frameworks do get results, they are often short term and lack the necessary capacity-building strategies that lead to sustained improvement or system transformation.

School and system transformation is unlikely to be achieved through punitive measures or narrow prescription. As argued throughout this book, transformation is more likely to occur through collaboration with and between schools (Harris et al, 2006a, 2006b). This is not to suggest that we fall into the trap of polarising competition versus collaboration. It is perfectly possible to have both but only in a system that offers both challenge and support, and does not encourage high standards to be achieved in one school at the expense of another. In a system rapidly moving towards post-standardisation,

2 See www.primaryreview.org.uk.

we cannot choose between collaboration and competition, they must now both connect for the public good (Hargreaves, 2007).

It is now a case of schools simultaneously building their internal capacity while supporting the capacity building of others. This internal capacity between and within schools will need to be deliberately and purposefully constructed (Chapter 8). Without continued attention to capacity building there is a danger that any form of leadership, no matter how effective in the short term, is unlikely to be sustained or sustainable. In schools that are in difficulty, capacity building is needed even more.

Turnaround leadership

Leadership on its own is unlikely to turn around the fortunes of a school in difficulty (Harris, 2006). Such schools have often tried a whole range of different initiatives, ideas and interventions only to be left disappointed and disillusioned. Most often these interventions and initiatives prove to be an unhelpful distraction that competes for precious time, energy and resources. The end result is a ' "perpetual carousel" where schools may move up and down with depressing regularity' (Hargreaves and Fink, 2006).

Patterns of school performance can remain stubbornly resistant to change. Fullan (2006:1) argues that in order to raise the *economic bar and close the income gap* we need to focus on social justice, health and well-being and economic development. He notes, 'Sick education systems mirror sick societies, not only because they directly affect one another but because the internal dynamics of diseased systems are similar'. In short, he argues that the real reform agenda is societal improvement rather than school improvement.

Despite the recognition of a powerful relationship between social and educational disadvantage and school performance (Berliner, 2005) there is still a tendency to continue to seek 'quick fix' solutions for schools in difficulty. As Hargreaves and Fink (2006) point out, the 'failing' school is a prime candidate for 'planned discontinuity' where there are the twin pressures of addressing poor performance while building the capacity for improvement.

There are examples of 'failing' schools that have been turned around by a charismatic new leader (Harris et al, 2006a, 2006b). In the majority of failing or under-performing schools, a new leader is almost always the first step taken in efforts to turn around their fortunes (Murphy and Meyers, 2008).

Unfortunately, such leaders, where they exist, are unable to meet the needs of so many schools in the system that are in difficulty. Also the evidence shows that many new heads rarely stay for the long term in such school contexts. There is a greater turnover of heads in schools in challenging circumstances because the leadership challenges they face are so acute and relentless (Harris et al, 2006a, 2006b). Therefore a different solution is required.

The *revolving door* of leadership succession not only creates huge instability within schools, particularly those in greatest need of stability, but also lays the blame for failure with individuals. Poor or inadequate leadership becomes the focus of attention rather than the deep endemic social problems facing the school and its community. If the head or principal fails to turn around a school, this failure is personalised and made public. The popular media are quick to highlight the fate of yet another leader who has not met expectations. So the head or principal leaves and the same solution to the problem is sought. This time, all the school needs is the *right type* of leader to turn around its performance, the *right individual* to make everything better.

And so the cycle continues. Leadership failure upon successive failure is personalised and individualised. Instead of seeing leadership as a shared organisational responsibility, it is viewed narrowly as an individual set of traits or capabilities. Much like the football manager of a poorly performing team, responsibility is directed one way and one way only. The consequences of poor performance are the same. But if you select managers or school leaders on the basis of individual capability or personality, the outcome is inevitable. It is what leaders *do* rather than *who they are* that matters most.

Leaders of struggling schools, like managers of struggling teams, are expected to be 'superheroes', able to manufacture improvement through the sheer force of character, charisma and will. Their schools are expected to perform like schools in affluent areas but without any of the social capital or economic advantages. It is not surprising that these leaders often burn out or leave the school in the same state of crisis that they inherited.

A new conceptualisation of leadership is needed to break the cycle – where leadership is seen 'as the collective capacity to do useful things', and where leadership responsibility is *widely shared* beyond the head or principal (Senge, 1990:834). This viewpoint is premised on the central idea that contemporary organisations require collaboration and teamwork on a scale not required before. This 'new leadership' is about deep involvement in leadership practice and collective capacity building. As Drath and Palus (1994) point out:

> When you do not see dominance and social influence as the basic activities of leadership, you no longer think of leadership predominantly in terms of leaders (people who influence others) and followers (people who are influenced). Instead you can think about leadership as a process in which everyone in a community or group is engaged. This is a way of viewing leadership as part of a context.

Organisations seeking this collective capability need to go beyond leadership as an individualised achievement towards creating a more socially distributed capability. This alternative leadership is one where leadership capability is not just human capital or the sum total of individual leadership capabilities. Instead leadership capability is social capital, the sum total of organisational and community capacity.

It is the central proposition of this book that effective school leadership equates with capacity building. It argues that capacity-building approaches are most likely to generate the foundation for improved performance in schools and school systems, and that this is best secured through broad-based, distributed leadership. It also suggests that the current solutions proposed to the crisis in school leadership are short term, insular and primarily designed to retain, at all costs, the school leadership structures of today rather than to create the leadership structures of tomorrow.

In search of solutions

Whatever the contributors to the current crisis, it is clear that school leadership demands urgent and immediate attention. In stark economic terms, there is a supply-side imbalance, which will become more severe over the next five years. Governments and policy makers are aware of this problem and in their various ways are seeking generic and localised solutions.

In England, the 'National College for School Leadership has been asked to provide formal advice to the Secretary of State' about a range of possible ways forward (NCSL, 2006). The NCSL proposals cover a three-year period, although they openly acknowledge that the problem is more long term.

There are a range of proposed solutions under consideration and development. These include a *fast track* to headship for candidates who show potential and ability. In other sectors, fast-track programmes exist and work effectively and ensure a steady throughput of motivated and capable young leaders. Other solutions include better *succession planning*, which means the long-term preparation of leaders, ultimately creating a leadership pool from which to draw future leaders (Fink, 2006). In addition, certain under-represented groups will be actively targeted for leadership positions, i.e. women, black and ethnic minority groups. The main aim is to swell the current pool of potential heads from sources, yet untapped, or under-represented.

More radical solutions include securing heads from other parts of the public sector to work in schools. If there is a shortage of leaders in one area of the public sector, why not move them from other areas of the public or private sectors where such shortages are not experienced? Surely good leadership is simply good leadership whichever context or setting. It does have a certain pragmatic logic. But it only works if you define school leadership in terms of management tasks and responsibilities.

Conversely, if you want leaders of learning, then a background in education is essential. Evidence would suggest that professional knowledge plus an understanding of context is particularly important for effective leadership and that leadership, rather than management, is not easily transferred between different contexts or settings. In the National Health Service in England, employing leaders from other sectors (e.g. business, the army) was attempted, proved to be unsuccessful and was subsequently abandoned almost overnight.

A core aspect of the NCSL's succession planning work has been to seek local solutions and strategies through collaboration at a local level. The early signs are that this is working. Another solution to the leadership crisis involves stretching the existing leadership capacity in the system even further. Many heads are now leading more than one school. This model is currently operating in a growing number of schools in England and operates in other countries such as the Netherlands, where heads automatically preside over more than one school. There is evidence that this approach, in England, is showing some positive benefits: and that the longer term consequences for the 'home school' of the head being absent is not as detrimental as it was feared (Matthews, forthcoming) to be. It is also questionable how far this finite resource of executive head teachers can be stretched.

The majority of solutions identified to address the supply-side problem are premised on refilling the empty leadership posts in schools as quickly and cost-effectively as possible. The current situation is not being seen as an important opportunity to rethink leadership structures and practices. Rather it appears to be a problem to be solved, a fault-line to be adjusted, an imbalance to be recalibrated. But is replacing the existing leadership structures the right thing to do?

There seems to be little dissent from the position that it is the right thing to do. What would be the consequences of not filling the head teacher vacancies in schools? Well, it could be an opportunity to rethink leadership practices and a way of looking at alternative models of leadership. Are we so sure that the current leadership structures in our schools are still the best structures for twenty-first-century schooling? If not, why aren't we replacing them more quickly?

This is not to suggest that we ignore the leadership crisis, or pretend that the issues facing schools without a formal leader are insubstantial. They are not. Neither is it to suggest that we immediately dismantle and disband existing leadership structures in our schools, creating even more chaos and confusion. However, the current position offers an opportunity to trial, refine and test new approaches to leadership. It is important that we take it.

Distributing leadership

The current position offers policy makers and practitioners the opportunity to think radically and creatively about leadership practice in schools. It offers an opportunity to revisit the 'how' of school leadership, and also the 'why'. Are we really sure that current leadership structures and practices in schools are more than 'good enough'?

An independent study into school leadership in England (DfES, 2007) concluded that there was a need to transform school leadership in schools, in order to ensure that leaders are equipped to embrace and deliver for the future. Their recommendations for change included diversifying leadership models in order to promote new and emerging leadership practice proactively. They recommended that there should be 'a national programme to support schools seeking to move towards new models and the need to remove key legal and regulatory barriers to the development of new models' (p 11). The report also recommended the need to 'distribute responsibility with accountability in order to facilitate greater distributed leadership'.

One of the strongest themes to emerge from the report was the theme of *distributing leadership*. The research suggested that there was a general consensus among school leaders, staff and other stakeholders of the need to distribute leadership in schools and to develop staff and nurture talent throughout the organisation. They also found that although some school leaders genuinely believed that they were distributing leadership, the feedback from teachers and support staff suggested this was not the case. As later chapters show, distributed leadership can only be achieved by deliberately creating and orchestrating the internal conditions in which distributed leadership can function.

Overall, the central message from the PWC study is the need *for broader and distributed leadership in schools*, which implies more than succession planning, or simply generating more head teachers or principals in the system (DfES, 2007:8). But what is distributed leadership? The next chapter focuses on distributed leadership in some depth.

Chapter 3

Distributed leadership

> Leadership does not have to be, nor should it be, the function of someone specifically designated as holding formal office.
>
> (Obolensky, 2008)

Introduction

It is not the intention of this book to trace the history of the emergence of ideas relating to distributed leadership. This task has been undertaken very ably by others (e.g. Spillane and Zoltners Sherer, 2004; Gronn, 2000; Spillane, 2006). Rather the intention is to explore what is meant by distributed leadership, what it looks like in practice and what difference, if any, it makes to organisational change and development.

In summary, broad-based, deep, distributed leadership in schools is viewed as:

> . . . a set of functions or qualities shared across a much broader segment of the school community that encompasses teachers and other professionals and community members both internal and external to the school. Such an approach imposes the need for school communities to create and sustain broadly distributed leadership, systems, processes and capacities. (Copland, 2003:376)

The central argument of the book is that distributed leadership is at the heart of a much needed and long overdue reconceptualisation of school leadership practice. It suggests that distributed leadership, as an idea, is powerful for two reasons: firstly, it has the potential to free schools from the current rigidity and inflexibility of existing leader-ship structures and secondly, it has the potential to connect the practice of leadership more closely to teaching and learning.

This potential is illustrated clearly in the 'Raising Achievement Transforming Learning Project' (RATL). This project has involved over 300 schools in England in seeking new and innovative ways of working together. This work has resulted in alternative models of leadership practice within and across schools. The initial results of this programme are positive, and the indicators of success are encouraging. The evaluation report highlights the need to share leadership responsibility even *more widely within and across schools* in order to sustain progress (Hargreaves and Shirley, 2007).

This book draws upon evidence from schools and from research to address three fundamental questions:

- what is distributed leadership?
- what does distributed leadership look like in schools?
- what difference, if any, does distributed leadership make to organisational and individual learning?

In addressing these three questions, the book will draw upon the latest research evidence and will integrate examples of practice to illustrate how schools are distributing leadership. Drawing on the work of Jim Spillane and his colleague (Spillane and Zoltners Sherer, 2004), this book will take a *deliberative* and *normative* perspective on distributed leadership rather than a theoretical or analytical stance. It will identify, describe and illuminate distributed leadership practice and take a critical look at its relationship with organisational change and development.

A tipping point?

In his work Gladwell (2000) argues that change happens not grad-ually but at one dramatic moment. His theory suggests that there are moments when we reframe the way we think about the world (Gladwell, 2000). At the heart of the book is the firm belief that the leadership models of the past are simply inadequate for the edu-cational challenges of the future. The central premise is that we need alternative leadership models that are both empirically grounded and practically possible. In terms of leadership practice in schools, it is suggested that we are at a 'tipping point'.

Global change is fuelling the demand for alternative organisational forms. The climate is right for alternative models of leadership practice to emerge. For some, this is also a moment to argue for the end of leadership as an idea. Writers like Lakomski (2005) have long argued that it is questionable whether leadership is the correct label or descriptor for the type of activity or influence that is considered to drive organisational change.

Her work challenges the premise that leadership is a natural entity or essence within the organisation, proposing instead that leadership is a distraction from exploring the real workings of organisational practice. She calls into question whether our 'taken for granted understanding of leadership . . . squares with how leaders and organisations really work given what we know about human cognition and information processing' (Lakomski, 2005:139). Her work has consistently argued that leadership is a label applied to behaviour that could just as easily be labelled as something else.

If we accept that leadership is the *right label* then it is important to ask what exactly are we labelling. There is still a powerful relationship between leadership and certain individual behaviours, traits and characteristics (Fullan, 2004). The romantic notion of the *hero leader* is one that prevails and persists in spite of countless examples of the organisational vulnerability of this form of leadership practice.

While the *hero leader* may seem superficially attractive to policy makers, we simply cannot afford to base serious system-wide reform and renewal upon this type of leadership. It is too dependent upon individual capability and capacity (Copland 2003). As Hargreaves and Fink (2006:95) argue 'in a complex, fast paced world, leadership cannot rest on the shoulders of the few'. It is their contention that sustainable leadership has to be distributed leadership, which is firmly centred on learning.

So if we are at a *tipping point* where the prevailing climate is particularly receptive, if not eager, for an alternative conceptualisation of leadership, what does it look like? Across schools and school systems we are seeing the patterns of leadership shift to more distributed forms. There is no doubt that distributed leadership is at the heart of the current discourse about leadership practice in schools. It is the leadership idea of the moment and its popularity shows little signs of receding.

Distributed leadership is currently filling the vacuum left by countless leadership texts reiterating the same tired orthodoxies about school leadership. Whatever one feels about distributed leadership, it has certainly created a new momentum of thinking about leadership practice in schools. Most importantly, it has given a renewed prominence to considerations of teacher leadership (Murphy, 2005) student leadership and community leadership, which have so often been dismissed, devalued and discounted in favour of more traditional and narrow conceptions of leadership.

The idea of teacher leadership embraces the core principles of distributed leadership because it is premised upon lateral, networked and fluid forms of leadership practice in schools (Leithwood et al, 2004; Harris, 2005). It suggests a more inclusive model of leadership practice that is not dependent on hierarchical leadership structures. Whether it delivers is another matter. Within schools, combinations of formal leadership will inevitably coalesce with informal leadership to produce different patterns of leadership practice.

The central point here is that vertical and lateral patterns of practice already exist in schools but in many cases the leadership potential of informal leadership is not being maximised. This is primarily because more attention is paid to the formal leadership activity rather than the informal. Distributed leadership is primarily concerned with the interactions in *both formal and informal* leadership and the way they produce different patterns of activity. As Spillane and Zoltners Sherer (2004) suggest, distributed leadership is a way of focusing upon leadership *as practice* as the co-production of knowledge, rather than leadership as role, position or a set of competences.

Testing the idea?

Before getting too carried away, we need to put distributed leadership under some scrutiny. The leadership field is very fond of new theories or labels for leadership, often produced without any recourse to empirical evidence. New leadership theories are formulated, packaged and successfully sold to schools without any empirical verification. All too often these leadership theories are no more than best guesses about leadership practice – weakly conceptualised and under-theorised.

Many new ideas about leadership are derived from retrospective, case study accounts of individual leadership practice and offer a highly subjective view. The book by Rudolph Giuliani about his experiences of the events of 11 September 2001 is one such example. It is a retrospective account of leadership in a crisis situation, very moving and humbling (Giuliani, 2002). Yet it remains an individual account, *a story* about leadership in action that is not intended to be validated or corroborated.

There are many such stories in the educational world that offer important insights about individual approaches to leading, but tell us little about the actual practice of leadership. So often they offer little more than *silver bullet* advice, which reinforces that leadership is what individuals do and that personal accounts of leadership are good proxies for empirical data.

Levin (2006) suggests that the knowledge base on leadership faces a problem, as there are 'many viewpoints in the field and very little solid research supporting them. Much of what parades as research is opinion garbed in the language of research'. So it is imperative that any consideration of distributed leadership or any other new model of leadership must be put to the theoretical and empirical test. We cannot simply accept that it is a good thing. As Gunter and Ribbins (2003:132) note:

> While distributed leadership tends to be seen as normatively a good thing, it has also been contested . . . most notably because of the complexities of who does the distribution and who is in receipt of distribution.

Distributed leadership should not simply be taken at face value as a *good thing*. There are critical questions about its relationship with organisational development and change that require serious empirical investigation (Harris, 2007b). While the emerging picture is positive, more work is needed (Silins and Mulford, 2002; Leithwood et al, 2006a, 2006b).

The book takes as its starting point that 'distributed leadership is a way of analysing and understanding leadership practice' (Spillane and Zoltners Sherer, 2004). However, it goes further by taking a deliberate *normative and descriptive stance* on distributed leadership. But what exactly do we mean by distributed leadership? It is clear that it means different things to different people, and there is confusion surrounding the concept (Harris, 2007b). Therefore the next section aims to explore the different interpretations and definitions. It aims to uncover what is meant by distributed leadership.

Definitions

In the popular educational press, distributed leadership has often been positioned in an oppositional way to vertical, hierarchical and formal leadership practices. It has been associated with the terms *lateral* and *informal leadership*, but its exact meaning has proved to be rather elusive.

Despite the widespread interest in the idea of *distributing leadership*, there have been competing and sometimes conflicting interpretations of the term. The definitions and understandings of distributed leadership extend from the normative to the theoretical and, by implication, the literature supporting the concept of distributed leadership is diverse and broad based (Bennet et al, 2003).

Within the existing literature it is clear that the idea of distributed leadership overlaps substantially with shared (Pearce and Conger, 2003), collaborative, democratic (Gastil, 1997) and participative (Vroom and Yago, 1998) leadership. This accumulation of allied concepts means that distributed leadership is often used in a shorthand way to describe any form of devolved, shared or dispersed leadership practice in schools. It is this *catch-all* use of the term that has resulted in both its misuse and its abuse.

It has also been pointed out that if leadership equates with influence, then inevitably all leadership is distributed. This is true but the way in which leadership is distributed, the patterns of distribution, are very important. Recent research by Hargreaves and Fink (2006) and Leithwood et al (2006a, 2006b; 2007) has shown that different patterns of distributed leadership are critical in achieving organisational improvement and change. A pattern of everyone leading at the same time is not one that is generally associated with organisational efficiency or effectiveness, but distributed leadership is often misunderstood to mean that *everyone leads*.

At the core of distributed leadership is the central notion that leadership is not the preserve of an individual but results from multiple interactions at different points in the organisation (Spillane, 2006; Harris, 2006). This conception of leadership moves beyond trying to understand leadership through the actions and beliefs of *single leaders* to understanding leadership as a dynamic organisational entity. As Spillane and Zoltners Sherer (2004) suggest, distributed leadership *is* 'constituted through the interaction of leaders, teachers, and the situation as they influence instructional practice'. It is a form of leadership practice that involves many organisational members.

Here organisational influence and decision making is governed by the interaction of individuals, rather than individual direction.

Not a new idea

To fully understand distributed leadership requires some consideration of its genesis. It is certainly not a new idea. Initially, the term was used by an Australian psychologist (Gibb, 1954) to try and understand the operation and dynamics of the processes that influenced the work of a variety of formal and formal groups. In seeking to identify ways of measuring patterns of influence in small group or team settings, a distinction was made between *focused* and distributed leadership.

Focused leadership meant that the activity was concentrated on one person while distributed leadership was simply a short-hand way for saying that the leadership was shared or distributed with individuals taking the lead at various times. In distributed leadership, influence would shift as different individuals emerged to be influential. As Youngs (2007:3) points out, distributed leadership is also a form of relational leadership. Relational leadership involves being attuned to and in touch with the intricate web of inter- and intra-relationships that influence an organisation. As Wenger (1998) highlights, it is about the meaning and identity that are created when people *work together*.

Early work in the field of educational administration also reinforced that leadership was not limited to executive positions and that it might be carried out by any member of the organisation. Barnard (1968) was one of the first writers to propose that leadership influence does not only travel in a downward direction but *flows throughout* the organisation, spanning levels and circulating up and down hierarchies.

Other writers, for example Shelley (1960), used the term to describe a difference of opinion among team members about the role of the leader; here the term served as a contrast to *focused leadership* in which there is clear consensus regarding the leadership hierarchy. From this perspective, it could be posited that distributed leadership is something to be avoided in organisations because it leads to a lack of stability, predictability and security among members. However the evidence to support this position is limited.

In the field of organisational dynamics the term has been used as a synonym for a 'bossless team' or a 'self-managed team' (Barry, 1991).

This work suggests that distributed leadership is a collection of roles and behaviours that can be split apart, shared, rotated and used sequentially or concomitantly. This essentially means that at any one time, multiple leaders can exist in a team, with each leader assuming a complementary leadership role. Unlike leadership substitute approaches, where attempts are made to reduce or eliminate the need for a leader, the distributed leadership model emphasises the *active cultivation and development* of leadership abilities within the organisation. The core assumption is that each member has leadership capability that will be needed by the group at some time.

The main message here is that leadership capability and capacity is not fixed, but can be extended and developed. This means that in schools, as different people seek and are tacitly or openly granted leadership functions, a *dynamic pattern* of distributed leadership gradually takes over. Over time, the leadership needs of the organisation will inevitably shift and change. These needs are unlikely to be met without fluid, flexible and adaptive sources of leadership.

Within a distributed leadership model, the responsibility of those in formal leadership roles in schools is to ensure that informal leaders have the opportunity to lead at appropriate times and are given the necessary support to make changes or to innovate (Harris, 2003). Distributed leadership does not imply that the formal leadership structures within organisations are removed or redundant. Instead, it is assumed that there is a *powerful relationship* between vertical and lateral leadership processes. It also means that those in formal leadership roles are the gatekeepers to distributed leadership practice in their schools. They purposefully create conditions for distributed leadership to happen and to flourish.

The next three chapters look at distributed leadership through three different lenses – the theoretical, the empirical and the practical.

Chapter 4

Distributed leadership
The theory

There is nothing more powerful than an idea whose time has come.
(Victor Hugo, *Les Misérables*, 1862)

Unlike many other leadership ideas, distributed leadership is located within a strong theoretical frame. The most contemporary interpretation of distributed leadership theory is that provided by Spillane (2006). His work has drawn upon distributed cognition and activity theory to develop a theory of distributed leadership practice. Spillane et al (2001:20) suggest that distributed leadership is best understood as 'practice distributed over leaders, followers and their situation and incorporates the activities of multiple groups of individuals'. This implies a social distribution of leadership where the leadership function is 'stretched over the work of a number of individuals and the task is accomplished through the interaction of multiple leaders' (2001: 20). This theoretical framing implies that the social context, and the inter-relationships therein, is an integral part of the leadership activity.

In his book, *Cognition in the Wild*, Edward Hutchins looks at the work of a navigation team on a US Navy ship. His analysis reveals that each action, such as bringing the vessel into port, is informed by the way that the team act as a cognitive and computational system. He proposes that the action of observing and describing navigational tasks reveals that there is a group of individuals who in interaction with each other are learning, communicating and acting collectively. They are in essence a learning system, a form of distributed cognition or learning in action. He notes, 'it is possible for a team to organize its behavior in an appropriate sequence without there being a global script or plan anywhere in the system. Each crew member only needs to know what to do when certain conditions are produced in the environment' (Hutchins 1995:15).

While the world of the school may be very different from that of a naval ship, as large organisations they both share complex social systems and the need for communication and learning to be distributed across the system. Distributed cognition implies that learning takes place through interactions within and across various teams. Distributed leadership similarly implies that the *practice of leadership* is one that is shared and realised within extended groupings and networks: some of these groupings will be formal while others will be informal and, in some cases, randomly formed.

In short, where teachers and other staff are working together to solve particular sets of pedagogical problems, they will occupy a leadership *space* within the school and will be engaging in leadership practice, which will impact upon others. The point is that distributed leadership is not restricted to any particular pattern but is arranged within the organisation in order to respond to particular problems and issues as they emerge.

In his work, Peter Gronn (2000:226) sees distributed leadership as an 'emergent property of a group or a network of interacting individuals'. Here leadership is a form of *concerted action*, which is about the additional dynamic that occurs when people work together or is the product of conjoint agency. The implication, largely supported by the teacher development and school improvement literature, is that organisational change and development are enhanced when leadership is broad-based, and where teachers have opportunities to collaborate and to actively engage in change and innovation (Little, 1990; Hopkins, 2001; MacBeath, 1998; Murphy, 2005).

A web of leadership

It was not until the late 1990s and early 2000s that the contemporary concept of distributed leadership was defined i.e. *'as being a web of leadership activities and interactions stretched across people and situations'* (Camburn et al, 2003; Heller and Firestone, 1995; Copland, 2003; Spillane and Zoltners Sherer, 2004). The work by Spillane et al (2001) and Spillane and Zoltners Sherer (2004) in particular highlights linkages between distributed leadership practice in elementary schools and improvements in the quality of teaching and learning in particular subject areas.

Unlike many other contemporary leadership theories or models, distributed leadership is a form of leadership not restricted by organisational or structural constraints. Rather it is a model primarily concerned with leadership practices and *interactions*, rather than the *actions* of individuals in a leadership position or role. It is also a model of leadership that implies *broad-based involvement* in the practice of leadership i.e. involving teachers, other professionals, students, parents and the wider community in decision making (Harris and Lambert, 2003).

Distributed leadership assumes a set of 'direction-setting' influences potentially 'enacted by people at all levels rather than a set of personal characteristics and attributes located in people at the top' (Fletcher and Kaufer, 2003:22). Non-person sources of influence also may be included in this concept such as, for example, Jermier and Kerr's (1997) *substitutes for leadership*, moving us toward a view of leadership as an organisation-wide phenomenon (Pounder et al, 1995).

Changing structures: crossing boundaries

Leadership in both the private and public sector has undergone a radical shift in recent years. In the private sector, in particular, leadership structures have been frequently, possibly too frequently redesigned to meet changing needs. The trend towards flatter matrix structures rather than hierarchies is increasingly becoming the norm. So reorganisation is endemic. For example the average firm can expect reorganisation every three years.

However, the process of restructuring is not an end in itself; it is whether this process results in more effective forms of leadership practice. As Wageman et al (2008) note:

> . . . in the longer term, the key to success lies in the ability to create and manage effective teams, to stimulate an environment in which innovation and knowledge sharing are nor just given lip service and to communicate complex concepts of strategy comprehensibly to a wider stakeholder group.

Within both the private and the public sectors, distributed leadership is becoming the prevalent model. There is an increasing focus on leadership at all levels and an increasing recognition of the need to build broad-based leadership capacity in order to survive.

A major study of effective leadership in England concluded that 'well-executed distributed leadership is a key feature of effective

models of leadership' (DfES, 2007:89). There was a general consensus amongst the stakeholders that contributed to the study of a
need for greater distributed leadership in schools, coupled with
structures that facilitate a great focus on teamwork. Collarbone
(2005) emphasises that distributed leadership is a necessity given the
new challenges for schools: she notes:

> . . . leadership in many of our schools remains vested in the
> hands of one person, and in most of our schools with just a small
> number of individuals, and this continues to be based around
> existing hierarchies. The new demands upon schools will require
> new ways of working and to make them work will require a
> greater degree of team working and more widely distributed
> leadership authority. (Collarbone, 2005:827)

There would seem to be some support from the literature for the idea
that distributing leadership has the potential to secure organisational
change. However, distributing leadership may not be as straightforward as it sounds. Distributing leadership inevitably implies
crossing or dismantling strong structural and cultural boundaries
within an organisation. It implies thinking about leadership in
a new way that takes us from a *person solo* to a *person plus* perspective
on leadership. Spillane et al (2001) call this the *leadership plus*
aspect.

It is also clear that organisations have different internal capacities
to develop, grow and innovate and that these capacities are heavily
dependent on different patterns of leadership activity. There is
increasing evidence to suggest that certain patterns or configurations
of distributed leadership offer greater potential for organisational
change and development (Leithwood et al, 2007). In short, distributing leadership means the active formation and facilitation of leadership activity and connection at different points within and across the
school. Taking a distributed perspective on leadership will require
active facilitation and the creation of the internal conditions in
which it will thrive.

Schools as organisations present considerable challenges to new
practices and ways of working. Their structures can be inflexible and
their cultures resistant to the adoption of different forms of operation. It would appear that there are three main barriers that make
distributing leadership and the sustaining of learning communities
in schools difficult to achieve.

- *Distance:* As schools grow and become more complex organisations through various partnerships and collaborations with other schools, the issue of distance makes it more difficult for teams to meet and problem solve. The physical space and distance can be a barrier to distributing leadership as the geographic separation makes it more difficult for teachers to connect. The challenge for schools, therefore, is to provide new, alternative, possibly ICT-based solutions to break the barrier of distance and to seek alternative forms of communication.

- *Culture:* Distributing leadership essentially means a shift in culture away from the *top-down* model of leadership to a form of leadership that is more organic, spontaneous and ultimately more difficult to control. It means a departure from a view of leadership that resides in one person to a more sophisticated and complex notion of leadership as a distributed property. The challenge for schools is to see leadership as an *organisational resource* that is maximised through interactions between individuals, and that leads to problem solving and new developments.

- *Structure:* The way schools are currently organised presents a set of barriers to distributing leadership. The structure of schooling is still dominated by compartmentalising subjects, pupils and learning into discrete but manageable boxes. Distributing leadership implies the erosion of these artificial barriers and implies a more fluid way of schools operating. The challenge for schools is to find ways of removing those organisational structures and systems that restrict organisational learning. As we will see in Chapters 7 and 8, schools are already dismantling structural barriers.

So where does this take us? Firstly, it requires those in formal leadership roles to create the cultural and structural conditions or spaces where distributed leadership can operate best and flourish. Secondly, it asks those in formal leadership positions to develop informal leaders and to maximise opportunities to develop their leadership potential. Thirdly, it implies a move away from the *leader–follower* relationship, to a focus upon the interactions between different leaders of various types and at various levels within the organisation.

The *leader–follower* relationship implies a power imbalance, whereas in distributed leadership *all relationships* are important and leadership can only be enacted if there is mutual trust and agreement about the way tasks are undertaken. Finally, distributed leadership necessitates that we scrutinise the relationship between distributed leadership and learning, focusing particularly on whether and in what form distributed leadership can promote positive learning outcomes. It is the relationship between distributed leadership and learning that will be considered in the next chapter.

Chapter 5

Distributed leadership
The evidence

> It is not the strongest of the species that survive, not the most intelligent, but those most responsive to change.
>
> (Charles Darwin, *The Origin of Species*, 1909).

Introduction

Over the last half-century, a great deal has been written about the importance of leadership in relation to organisational performance. It would seem that no modern concept has been more powerfully received in the consciousness of those concerned with school reform and improvement than leadership. The contemporary literature highlights and reinforces the importance of leadership in generating and sustaining school development and change (Day et al, 1999; Fullan, 2001). Academics from different fields of study have concluded that leadership is a *central variable* in the equation that defines organisational development success (Murphy et al, 2006).

Effective leadership, primarily in the guise of the school head teacher or principal, has long been identified with school success, and has been seen as the central ingredient in securing higher levels of student achievement (Murphy, 1988; Leithwood et al, 2004; Marzano et al, 2005). Over the last three decades, the sheer volume of literature on the subject is testament to the popularity of leadership and its tenacity in the face of some strong opposition. It is clear from many empirical studies that leadership is a powerful determinant of subsequent organisational success and improvement (Townsend, 2007; Reynolds et al, 1995; Stoll and Fink, 1996). The empirical evidence about the *exact* nature of the relationship between leadership and learning is, however, less clear.

An array of researchers over the years have reinforced that there is no best way of leading. They have also shown that effective leadership is context-related and context-specific. Ultimately the leadership of the head or principal is mediated by school operations and classroom activities (Murphy et al, 2006). The evidence suggests that the effects of leadership on pupil learning outcomes are largely indirect for sources of leadership *outside the classroom* – head teachers, inspectors, governors, secretaries (Hallinger and Heck, 1996).

In order for these sources of leadership to impact upon student outcomes, they need to exercise some form of positive influence on the work of other colleagues, particularly teachers, as well as on the status of key conditions or characteristics of the organisation: school culture, for example. These are the intervening moderating and mediating influences, or variables that make it more or less likely that leadership impacts upon learning (Day et al, 2007).

Heads and principals have a direct relationship or influence upon those school and classroom variables, which, in turn, have a direct influence on pupil learning. How we think about the variables intervening between leaders and students depends, in some measure, on the size and type of the school organisation. In a small primary school, for example, many heads typically have significant teaching roles and have contact with pupils in the classroom. In large secondary schools, the influence of heads or principals on pupils' academic learning will almost always be *mediated* through other adults.

We know that leadership acts as a catalyst for change within schools. This doesn't mean that leadership is inherently good or virtuous but rather that it is a force that can provide organisational momentum and energy. As highlighted earlier, Leithwood et al (2006a, 2006b) claim that 'school leadership is second only to classroom instruction as an influence on pupil learning'. They base this claim on evidence about leadership effects from large-scale quantitative studies of overall leader effects, which conclude that the combined direct and indirect effects of school leadership on pupil outcomes are small but *educationally significant*. While leadership explains only *5 to 7 per cent* of the variation in pupil learning across schools, this amount of explained variation is actually about *one-quarter* of the total across-school variation (12 to 20 per cent) explained by all school-level variables, after controlling for pupil intake or background factors.[1]

---

1 Evidence justifying this point has been reported by Creemers (1996:218).

Leithwood et al (2006) conclude from this evidence that leadership has a *very significant effect* on the quality of the school organisation and on pupil learning. They note:

> . . . leadership serves as a catalyst for unleashing the potential capacities that already exist in the organisation. Those in leadership roles have a tremendous responsibility to 'get it right'.

In summary, those in formal leadership roles in schools have an indirect effect on pupil learning but a direct effect on the organisational conditions that support learning (Harris, 2005). There is emerging evidence that broadening or distributing leadership can positively impact on these organisational conditions. The next section will explore this evidence base in more depth.

Distributed leadership and organisational learning: the evidence

As noted earlier, new labels and adjectives for leadership appear on an almost daily basis. The leadership industry is replete with redundant leadership ideas and rejected leadership theories. As soon as one theory disappears, another immediately replaces it, raising some questions about the legitimacy of the knowledge base. Many of these theories are simply constructed and promulgated with little consideration of whether they are grounded in the practicalities and realities of schools, or whether there is any link to learning.

If we accept that leadership is a core ingredient of organisational success, shouldn't we be asking *what forms of leadership generate and sustain organisational improvement?* In other words, *what evidence do we have that distributed leadership is more likely than other forms of leadership to result in positive student learning outcomes?* Here we hit the first problem. There is limited evidence about the *direct* relationship between distributed leadership and learning. We have, at present, limited systematic, detailed evidence about this relationship, although what is emerging is encouraging (e.g. Camburn et al, 2003; Spillane and Diamond, 2007; Leithwood et al, 2007).

The evidence base on distributed leadership is diverse. It is located in the literature on organisational change, organisational effectiveness, school improvement, professional learning communities and teacher leadership. Youngs (2007:2) suggests that there are 32 studies of distributed leadership practice from 2002 to 2007. A quick glance at these studies reveals that they range from small case study accounts of distributed leadership practice (e.g. Court, 2003; Macbeath, 2005) to findings from teacher leadership projects (e.g. Crowther et al, 2002), to more general studies of effective leadership, to studies of literacy (Timperley, 2005).

In many of these studies, distributed leadership has not been the central focus of the empirical enquiry. Only four studies stand out as being large scale and explicitly focused on examining the relationship between distributed leadership and organisational or learning outcomes (Camburn et al, 2003; Leithwood et al, 2004 and 2007; Spillane et al, 2003 and 2007; and Spillane and Zoltners Sherer, 2004). These studies will be explored in more detail later in the chapter.

Distributed leadership and organisational change

Even though the literature on distributed leadership is so diverse, it does offer some interesting insights into the relationship with organisational change. Work by Graetz (2000) offers a view of distributed leadership as a positive channel for organisational change. He notes that 'organisations most successful in managing the dynamics of loose–tight working relationships meld strong personalised leadership at the top with distributed leadership'. Similarly Gold et al (2002) in their study of ten 'outstanding' school leaders, point towards the development of *leadership capacity* within the school as a key lever of success.

The literature on networked learning communities and professional learning communities demonstrates that distributed leadership is an important component in securing improved learning. Stoll and Seashore Louis (2007:2) suggest 'that professional learning communities have the capacity to promote and sustain the learning of professionals in a school with the collective purpose of enhancing student learning'. They point out that the forms of leadership required to enhance learning are widely *distributed*. Lieberman (2007:201) highlights that when participants were involved in *sharing their leadership practice*, they felt ownership not only for their work but also for their peers. In their in-depth commentary on networked learning communities, Jackson and Temperley (2007:60) highlight that leadership of these groups is determined by 'purpose rather than rank'. They note that 'a networked learning community, just like a professional learning community, needs appropriate leadership and facilitation' (Jackson and Temperley 2007:52).

Research by Morrisey (2000) concludes that *extending* leadership responsibility beyond the principal is an important lever for developing effective professional learning communities in schools. A range of other studies (Portin, 1998) also point towards a positive relationship between organisational change and distributed forms of leadership practice.

The school improvement literature contains similar messages about the types of leadership that accompany positive change in schools. It has consistently underlined the importance of teacher involvement in decision-making processes, and the contribution of strong collegial relationships to positive school improvement and change (Townsend, 2007).

Judith Warren Little (1990) suggests that 'collegial interaction', at least, lays the groundwork for developing shared ideas and for generating forms of leadership that promote improvement. While Little's (1990) work does not refer to distributed leadership explicitly, it does point towards collaborative leadership processes among teachers. In her research work, Rosenholtz (1989) argues even more forcibly for teacher collegiality and collaboration as a means of generating positive change in schools. Her research concludes that effective schools 'have tighter congruence between values, norms and behaviours of principals and teachers', and that this is more likely to result in positive school performance. The work of Nias and her colleagues in English schools (Nias et al, 1989) provided similar conclusions. The implication from these empirical studies is that improvement is more likely to occur when there are opportunities for teachers to work together and to *lead* development and change.

There is an increasing body of evidence that points towards the importance of capacity building as a means of sustaining school improvement (e.g. Fullan, 2001; Sergiovanni, 2001). At the core of the capacity-building model, it has been argued, is distributed leadership along with social cohesion and trust. Leadership from this perspective resides in the human potential available to be released within an organisation. It is what Gronn (2000) terms 'an emergent property of a group or network of individuals in which group members pool their expertise'.

The term *formative leadership* has been developed on the belief that there are numerous leaders within the school (Lashway, 2003). Leadership is not reserved for those in formal position; rather their prime function is to facilitate learning opportunities for *other* staff so that they can develop into productive leaders. This is premised on the view that *teachers as leaders* emerge with the help of the administration. It is a deliberate form of capacity building within the school. It has been argued that successful organisations depend on multiple sources of leadership and that significant and continuous improvement happens when leaders, both at administrative and instructional levels, work collaboratively for school change (Lima, 2007).

Ogawa and Bossert (1995) suggest that the particular perspective from which leadership is viewed will determine the view of leadership. The authors argue that the dominant view of leadership has been a *technical-rational* perspective, where there are four basic assumptions that frame the understanding of leadership. The four underlying assumptions are that:

1   Leadership functions to influence organisational performance.
2   Leadership is related to organisational roles.
3   Leaders are individuals who contain certain attributes and act in certain ways.
4   Leaders operate within the organisational culture.

Using this perspective of leadership, leaders are inevitably confined to the upper-most levels of organisational hierarchies where goal attainment is the primary objective.

Ogawa and Bossert (1995) outline a view of organisations from the institutional perspective, where the function of leadership is social legitimacy and organisational survival. The authors describe leadership as follows: '. . . we treat leadership as a quality of organisations – a systemic characteristic. To find it, we submit, one must not look in one place or another but must step back and map leadership throughout organisations' (p 225). From this perspective, leadership must be more than one individual's actions: it must influence the entire system in which it occurs.

Studies in England (Harris, 2002), Norway and Australia (Gurr et al, 2005) confirm Ogawa and Bosert's conclusion by showing that improvement at the school level was achieved through involving a wide array of stakeholders in decision making and leadership. While the connections between distributed leadership and student outcomes were not explored directly, the leadership approaches adopted by the heads and principals in these successful schools could be characterised as widely distributed.

Interest in distributed leadership has also accumulated because of the expansion of different forms of collaboration between and across schools. In some regions of the Netherlands, schools are grouped together under one head teacher. In the current educational land-scape in England, different forms of distributed leadership are already emerging in schools in the form of executive head, co-headship, assistant heads and leadership teams that oversee two or three schools in federation or partnerships.

Within the growing number of school-to-school networks, it has been argued that distributed leadership may provide greater opportu-nities for members to learn from one another. A recent systematic review of the literature on the impact of networks on pupils, practi-tioners and the communities they serve concludes that networks offer opportunities for teachers to 'share, initiate and embed new practices' (Bell et al, 2006). While the direct link between networking and achievement was not forthcoming from this review of the research evidence, the data that does exist highlights a positive relationship between increased teacher collaboration both within and across schools and organisational development.

Less favourable perspectives

Less favourable perspectives on distributed leadership also exist in the literature. Many writers tend to polarise distributed forms of leader-ship against more conventional *focused* forms of leadership. The more contemporary literature highlights some of the difficulties associated with actively distributing leadership in schools.

It shows that there are certain barriers to overcome in order to achieve a model of distributed leadership, and that achieving dis-tributed leadership in practice is far from straightforward. For example, Timperley (2005) has pointed to possible drawbacks and caveats associated with a normative position on distributed leadership (also Colwell, and Hammersley-Fletcher, 2004). For example:

> While distributed leadership among teachers may be desirable, some caution needs to be sounded about the potential difficulties involved. Although formally appointed leaders do not auto-matically command respect and authority, teacher leaders may be particularly vulnerable to being openly disrespected and

disregarded because they do not carry formal authority. On the other hand, nomination of teacher leaders by colleagues may not realize potential expertise within the group because colleagues may select their leaders using other criteria.

(Timperley, 2005:412).

As noted earlier, it would be naïve to ignore the major structural, cultural, and micro-political barriers operating in schools that can make distributed forms of leadership difficult to implement. Distributed leadership may be considered too threatening to those in formal power positions, not only in terms of ego and perceived authority, but also because it places leaders in a vulnerable position, as they have to relinquish direct control over certain activities.

Current school structures may actually prevent teachers from attaining autonomy and taking on leadership roles. Also top–down approaches to distributed leadership, when not executed properly, can also be potentially damaging and nothing more than misguided delegation. Goldstein's (2004) study of the distribution of leadership to teachers for teacher appraisal conducted in a large urban district in the United States highlighted a number of barriers. This work showed that hierarchical norms, district leaders' expectations and attitudes, difficulties associated with evaluation and ambiguities surrounding the evaluation process were all challenges to leadership distribution.

Distributed leadership and learning

Despite some of the methodological difficulties associated with researching distributed leadership, there are major studies that point to benefits for learning. Leithwood and his colleagues in Canada conclude from their large-scale investigation that 'distributing a larger proportion of leadership activity to teachers has a positive influence on teacher effectiveness and student engagement'. They also note that teacher leadership has a significant effect on student engagement that far outweighs principal leadership effects after taking into account home family background (Leithwood and Jantzi, 2000).

In Tasmania, the Silins and Mulford (2002) studies of leadership effects on student learning provide some cumulative confirmation of the key processes through which more distributed kinds of leadership influenced student learning outcomes. Their work collected survey data from over 2,500 teachers and their principals. It concluded that 'student outcomes are more likely to improve when leadership sources are distributed throughout the school community and when teachers are empowered in areas of importance to them'.

In England, a smaller-scale study found positive statistical relationships between the extent of teachers' involvement in decision-making and student motivation and self efficacy (Harris and Muijs, 2004). This study explored the relationship between teacher involvement in decision making within the school, and a range of student outcomes. It was clear from the study that more distributed forms of leadership had a positive impact on certain student outcomes. Both teacher and student morale levels improved where teachers felt more included and involved in decision-making processes that related to the school's development.

The *Distributed Leadership Study* (Spillane et al, 2001; Spillane and Zoltners Sherer, 2004) remains the largest contemporary study of distributed leadership practice. This four-year longitudinal study, funded by the National Science Foundation and the Spencer Foundation, in the USA, is one of very few studies focusing on distributed leadership and instructional outcomes. The project was designed to make the *black box* of leadership more transparent through an in-depth analysis of leadership practice. The central argument underpinning the study is that distributed leadership is best understood as distributed practice *stretched over* the school's social and situational contexts.

The research, which focused on 13 elementary schools in Chicago, found that the task of instructional improvement engaged *multiple leaders* and that understanding the interplay between different leaders is crucial to understanding leadership practice. Their study concluded that the *school* rather than the individual leader is the most appropriate unit for thinking about the development of leadership expertise. It also concluded that intervening to improve school leadership may not be most optimally achieved by focusing on the individual formal leader and may not offer the best use of resources.

Another study by Copland (2003) looked at the improvement in 86 schools that were engaged in data-driven, whole school reform. All the schools had a strong commitment to introducing and implementing participatory leadership. The study found extensive staff involvement in the leadership of the schools and involvement at all levels in decision making.

Work by Camburn et al (2003) focused on approximately 1,000 elementary schools in the USA. This study looked at the distribution of formal roles and new roles generated from the three Comprehensive School Reform programmes. Also in the USA, work by Karen Seashore Louis et al (2007) has focused upon schools that have deliberately become involved in changing leadership patterns. The data is providing insights into how teachers and school leaders are reacting to calls for more shared or distributed leadership.

In Canada, a large-scale study is exploring distributed leadership in schools and districts (Leithwood et al, 2006a, 2006b). This work has focused on different patterns of leadership distribution and its impact on organisational performance. Findings to date suggest that head teachers and principals have a great deal of responsibility for making distributed leadership work in the school. The findings suggest that the success with which leadership is distributed to teachers depends crucially upon administrative initiative and willingness. Their research has shown that:

- principals or head teachers *encourage* distributed forms of leadership when they create problem-solving teams to substitute for administrative leadership;
- principals or head teachers often have to select teachers to take on leadership responsibilities and that their selection needs to be based upon knowing what teachers are capable of doing, but also the forms of professional development that would *benefit* teachers.

As highlighted earlier, one of the barriers to distributed leadership is how leadership distribution is viewed by principals and teachers. If it is viewed as delegation, it is likely to be met with resistance by teachers not wanting to undertake yet more work. If principals or heads equate distributed leadership with an erosion of their power, it will be perceived as threatening and therefore unlikely to happen.

Other influences that affect the distribution of leadership have been identified by (Murphy, 2005) as:

- resources (including enough time for all aspects of preparing for and participating in leadership roles);
- incentives and recognition (including monetary and non-monetary rewards such as public acknowledgements);
- role clarity (including an effort to avoid creating resentment among colleagues).

These influences are not only important to teachers, but would also be significant if leadership were distributed to support staff, parents and students also. The work of Leithwood et al, (2006a, 2006b; 2007) points to the fact that distributing leadership to others 'does not result in fewer demands upon those in formal leadership roles'. So it would seem that distributed leadership is not a way of alleviating pressure on those in formal leadership roles. Conversely, distributed leadership produces greater demands in terms of co-ordinating, orchestrating and supporting leadership activity. It requires those in formal leadership roles to actively create the organisational infrastructure where informal leaders emerge.

Patterns of distribution

The initial findings from the Leithwood et al (2007) study show that particular patterns of distributed leadership matter in terms of organisational performance. The findings also reveal that the effects and impact of distributed leadership on organisational outcomes depend upon the *pattern of leadership distribution*. This work high-lights two key conditions necessary for successful leadership distribution.

1   Leadership needs to be distributed to those who have, or can develop, the *knowledge or expertise* required to carry out the leadership tasks expected of them.
2   Effective distributed leadership needs to be *coordinated*, preferably in some planned way.

These conditions for successful leadership distribution are derived from Locke's (2002) *integrated model* of leadership. This model acknowledges both the reality and the virtues, in most organisations, of distributed leadership based on multiple forms of lateral (e.g. teacher-to-teacher) influence. The model also highlights the *inevitable* sources of vertical or hierarchical leadership in any successful organisation.

Gronn (2003) distinguishes between two distinct forms of distributed leadership. He labels these two forms *additive* and *holistic*. Additive forms of distribution describe an *uncoordinated* pattern of leadership, in which many different people may engage in leadership functions without making much, if any, effort to take account of the leadership efforts of others in their organisation. Locke's model suggests that such unplanned patterns of distributed leadership would do little to help the organisation develop or grow.

'Holistic' or 'person-plus' leadership (Spillane, 2006) refers to *consciously managed* and synergistic relationships among some, many, or all sources of leadership in the organisation. This form of distributed leadership assumes that the sum of leaders' work adds up to more than the parts. It is also assumed that there are high levels of *interdependence among those providing leadership* and that the influence attributed to their activities emerges from dynamic, multidirectional, social processes which, at their best, lead to learning for the individuals involved, as well as for their organisations (Pearce and Conger, 2003).

Gronn (2003) has suggested that concertive forms of distributed leadership may take three forms:

- *Spontaneous collaboration*: from time to time, groupings of individuals with differing skills and knowledge capacities, and from across different organisational levels *coalesce* to pool their expertise and regularise their conduct for duration of the task, and then disband.
- *Intuitive working relations*: this form of concertive distributed leadership emerges over time, '. . . as two or more organisational members come to rely on one another and develop close working relations', and as 'leadership is manifest in the shared role space encompassed by their relationship' (Gronn, 2003:657).
- *Institutionalized practice*: citing committees and teams as their most obvious embodiment, Gronn (2003) describes such *formalized structures* as arising from design, or through less systematic adaptation.

Some elaboration and refinement of Gronn's (2003) holistic forms of distributed leadership have been proposed by Leithwood et al (2007):

- *Planful alignment*: the tasks or functions of those providing leadership have been given prior thoughtful consideration by organisation members. Agreements have been worked out among the sources of leadership (principals, heads of department and teachers etc) about which leadership practices or functions are best carried out by which source. Although *alignment* is generally considered a good thing for organisations, positive contributions of this configuration to productivity cannot be automatically assumed.
- *Spontaneous alignment*: in this configuration, leadership tasks and functions are distributed with *little or no planning*, for example:

the principal assumes she will be responsible for modelling values that are important to the school, and everyone else makes the same assumption. Nevertheless, tacit and intuitive decisions about who should perform which leadership functions result in a fortuitous alignment of functions across leadership sources.

- *Spontaneous misalignment*: this configuration mirrors spontaneous alignment in the manner of leadership distribution, as well as its underlying values, beliefs and norms. However, the outcome is different or *less fortuitous* – misalignment (which may vary from marginal to extensive). Both short- and long-term organisational productivity suffer from this form of (mis)alignment. However, organisation members are not opposed, in principle, to either planful or spontaneous alignment, thus leaving open reasonable prospects for future productive alignment of one sort or another.

- *Anarchic misalignment*: this configuration is characterised by active rejection, on the part of some or many organisation leaders, of input from others about what they should be doing in their own sphere of influence. As a result, those leaders' units behave *highly independently*, competing with other units on such matters as organisational goals and access to resources. Actively rejecting the influence of others, however, stimulates considerable reflection about one's own position on most matters of concern.

Early findings by Leithwood et al (2007) suggest that *planful and spontaneous* patterns of alignment have the greatest potential for positive organisational change. Furthermore, 'planful alignment' seems more likely to contribute more than other patterns of alignment to long-term organisational productivity. The research found that both spontaneous misalignment and anarchic alignment are likely to have negative effects on short- and long-term organisational change and development.

But what does the planful alignment of distribution look like in practice? What contextual factors influence whether and how leadership is distributed? The next chapter explores distributed leadership in context.

Chapter 6

Distributed leadership in context

> The most important thing going forward is to break the boundaries between people so we can operate as a single intelligence.
>
> (Einstein)

Introduction

The current context is one of rapid and unprecedented change. The way organisations function, operate and relate to each other is dramatically altering. Whether in business, health or education the organisational structures of the past are unlikely to be the structures of the future. Technology, global communication and the sheer pace of change necessitate a radical and permanent organisational redesign. As Yeats suggests, the *centre cannot hold*. In a 24/7 world, we have to review our educational practices, structures and ways of working and question whether they remain fit for purpose.

The philosopher and sociologist Charles Taylor (2004) invented the term 'social imaginary' to describe the broad understanding people have of themselves, their collective life and their society. This constitutes taken-for-granted assumptions about the way things are and how they work. An 'imaginary' is not reality but rather our way of comprehending what reality is.

As Hedley Beare (2006) points out, for many years, people thought that the earth was the centre of the universe until Copernicus offered an alternative explanation. His suggestion that the planets revolved around the sun challenged firmly held beliefs about the primacy of the earth in the solar system. It challenged the medieval notion of the *great chain of being* and it violated the notion of authority and who ordains the way things are believed to be.

There has always existed a powerful educational 'imaginary' in operation, and Beare (2006) suggests that the one we are currently operating under belongs to the early twentieth-century model of *mass production* rather than the twenty-first-century model of *personalisation*. In every age, as Toffler (1985) suggests, there are powerful patterns and understandings of the way things are, even though there are forces demanding fundamental changes and a shift in thinking. In every age, certain patterns are favoured and replicated in business, government, and educational practices. Moving to a different 'imaginary' requires a paradigm shift, a radical rather than an incremental shift in thinking.

This type of shift is described as a departure or break from previous practice with the establishment of new ways of working. Such a break is accompanied by a period of planned discontinuity, where new practices bear little resemblance to previous practices. Companies who transform themselves tend to survive even the most hostile competition. In 1928 Motorola established itself as a company that specialised in car radios. Since then it has changed its fundamental business several times, and is now one of the leading providers of mobile technology.

In his work David Hargreaves uses the term 'educational imaginary' to represent how the educational world is currently understood and suggests that a 'new educational imaginary' is needed. His work suggests that educational practices need to change urgently in order to prepare young people for the twenty-first century. It also implies that a new kind of workforce with new skills may be needed to meet the changing global demand and to prepare young people for jobs that haven't even been thought of yet.

The New Workforce

The New Workforce (2005) by Harriet Hankin identifies five major trends that are transforming 'work' as we currently know and understand it. These trends will have a major impact on the way education is conceptualised and realised in the future. In summary, these five major trends are as follows:

- *Longevity*: people are living longer and want to be engaged in work or some related activities for longer. *How will these people be used to contribute to learning and education?* Could they comprise a level of expertise and experience that 'schools' (if they continue to be called schools) might utilise?

- *Varied household types*: the nature of households has shifted considerably. The nuclear family is no longer the predominant model, and the mobility and differentiation of family configuration will inevitably create additional demands on an education system geared to a different type of family unit. *How can 'schools' maximise the potential and opportunities of such societal changes?*
- *Generation gaps*: the baby boomers are getting older and with this will come additional demands on the younger generation in terms of care, health costs, etc. Those born after the year 2000 are millennials, or generation z. These two groups will have very different experiences, expectations and demands of education. *How will teachers from one generation meet the needs of generation z?*
- *Globalisation and diversity*: this issue has already been explored in some depth earlier in the book. *In a globalised world, how do 'schools' provide 24/7 education?* A recent analysis of the use of Facebook showed that on average most users accessed the site 30 times a day and that the majority of young people accessed the site at 2 am.
- *Higher purpose for the workforce*: working priorities are also being redefined and transformed. Monetary remuneration remains important but job satisfaction or fulfilment is more important than ever before. *How do 'schools' ensure that all staff at all levels are motivated and fulfilled throughout their careers?* It has been estimated that a young person starting work today will have 14 job changes before he or she is 38. The majority of under-25s have been in their present job for less than a year and will do jobs in the future that have not been thought of yet.

Such trends inevitably mean that the current organisational forms are unlikely to survive. But what of the new models of educational design, what will they look like? The new educational models of the future are in fact already here. They are currently emerging in our schools and school systems.

In the struggle to transform educational systems on a large scale, one thing is clear – our past attempts at large-scale reform have tended to constrain system-level change by focusing on competition, thus restricting the potential for innovation and knowledge creation within and between schools. While *informed prescription* may have taken us so far, it is a feature of an educational landscape that is fading fast. The new educational order is rapidly emerging: its direction is being set by schools working together and it is best characterised by networks and network learning.

Fullan (2006:16) argues that 'changing whole systems means changing the entire *context* in which people work', and it is clear that the current context is rapidly shifting. During the last decade, educational reform in many countries has been characterised by centrally driven, top–down strategies and an over-emphasis on accountability. There has been some success but the strategies have now stalled and performance has reached a plateau. As a recent result, policy directions have reflected a significant shift towards the decentralisation of decision-making and personalisation. To move beyond the plateau, as Fullan (2004) puts it, will require marrying the world of moral purpose and collective identity and by working together differently, with a goal of producing quality ideas and practices on an ongoing basis'. Consequently, recent policy shifts, particularly in England have started to value school-to-school networking, and to recognise the potential of networks, federations or collaborations as important levers in system transformation.

Collaboration and networks

Collaboration and accountability are currently partners in the pursuit of improved educational performance at the school and system level. They are uncomfortable bedfellows: schools find it difficult to reconcile the contradictory forces of competition and collaboration. However, it would appear that obsession with performance management, compliance, conformity and standardisation is beginning to waver as the expected results in performance have failed to materialise. The standards agenda is beginning to crumble and in its place is emerging a process of school transformation based on collaboration and networking. This principle is at the very heart of system redesign (Hargreaves, 2007).

Andy Hargreaves and Dean Fink (2006) note that 'creativity emerges by putting disparate ideas together or by connecting different and diverse minds, or both'. This connection can only be achieved through a structural realignment that favours *lateral capacity building* within and across schools that extends into the wider community. Collaboration and networking are the means of achieving system-wide transformation.

The Wisdom of Crowds by James Surowiecki (2004) demonstrates the power of collective thinking and problem solving. He proposes that 'aggregated individual thinking' gives us perspectives and ideas that would be absent using more linear, individual forms of thinking. In short, the potential for imaginative and creative solutions to problems is more likely to occur where there is *collective* rather than *individual* consideration.

Some collective decisions are likely to be the product of disagreement and contest rather than compromise. The test of any partnership or network must be its ability to withstand and accommodate dissent without imploding or fracturing. This resilience, in part, will depend on the quality of support that operates both inside and outside the network. It will also depend on the degree of trust and professional respect nurtured within the social architecture of the network. As Hargreaves and Fink (2006) point out, 'if network cells are weak – then they will not drive improved practices but will perpetuate indifferent ones'.

In the nomenclature of educational change, collaboration is often equated with good or positive change. While there is a wealth of evidence to support this position, it is not always the case. Much depends on the *type* of collaboration that teachers embark upon, the *purpose* of collaboration and the *structures* that support their collaborative activity. The same is true of networking. The *networking equals improvement* equation is heavily dependent of the way in which networking is instigated, developed and supported within and across schools. It is not a given.

Lurking in the dark shadows and recesses of the popular discourse about networks is the real possibility that certain types of collaboration between schools may be counterproductive. There are *contrived* networks that are formed just simply for the extra resources, and they subsequently dissipate and disband when other more profitable opportunities arise. There are *cosy* networks based on friendship groups or existing partnerships that manifest the telltale signs of inertia, because powerful personal relationships dictate and restrict their activity. There are *colluding* networks that work together to disguise the fact that very little is really happening.

Huxham and Vangen (2006) talk about 'collaborative inertia', where the outcomes from certain types of collaborative activity are negligible or non-existent. They also talk about 'collaborative thuggery', where manipulation and political activity replace shared decision-making. Undoubtedly, such networks exist, all masquerading as professional learning communities and receiving both resource and acclaim as a result. Superficially, they appear like any other networks but further scrutiny will expose a structural shell without substance.

In *The Rise of the Network Society*, Manuel Castells (1996) notes that the performance of a given network will depend on two fundamental attributes of the network: 'its *connectedness* that is its structural ability to facilitate noise-free *communication* between its components and its consistency that is the extent to which there is a sharing of interests between the network's goals and the goals of its components'. In the case of ineffective networks, they have neither the connectedness nor the cohesion to function properly. Such networks can hoard knowledge, limit innovation and hold others hostage for their expertise. Wenger (1998) suggests that most community disorders are of three general types:

- They do not function because of a lack of trust.
- There is no focus upon tangible outcomes in their early stages.
- They fail to install mechanisms for knowledge transfer and collaborative forms of problem solving.

Meaningful networks on the other hand are based on clearly shared goals, clear ways of communicating, internal cohesion and mutual trust. Such networks function as learning communities, which may be a rather grand way of saying that schools learn better together than separately. Essentially, the sum is greater than the parts.

It is clear that networks of schools do not exist in isolation from the wider system. Their effectiveness therefore is not a matter of internal development alone but also a matter of *how* they connect with other communities and constituencies. Schools in federations, partnerships and networks represent constellations of communities that encompass many groupings and cross many boundaries. Their power is significantly enhanced through the interconnections they make across the wider system. The form of leadership they represent is ultimately distributed.

Leading networks

Networks or networking are not new phenomena. Networks have always existed at both formal and informal levels at school and system level. It is argued that networks have the potential to outperform more traditional, vertically organised organisations and that flexibility and adaptability are the key ingredients of success (Castells, 1996).

The establishment of school-to-school networks is consistent with the idea of 'knowledge creation' (see Chapter 8), developed by Nonaka and Takeuchi (1995). This is premised on the notion that new ideas, research breakthroughs and applications arise anywhere in the sector, not just within the boundaries of formal R and D activities. Where practitioners lead and disseminate new ideas, it has been argued that they are central to the 'sparking, shaping, validating and spreading of innovation' (Bentley and Gillinson, 2007:4). As Chesbrough (2003) argues, 'it's about harnessing the most effective sources of innovation from wherever they are derived. This is not just about ideas – it is about their realisation'. In his model of *open innovation*, users are involved in shaping the service and are active participants in knowledge creation.

Certain principles need to be at the core of these school-to-school interactions.

- *Geographic distribution*: participants are likely to be geographically distributed. Therefore the system must support multiple modes of interaction to accommodate the preferences and learning styles of the individual members.
- *Purpose, mission, vision and values*: the infrastructure must facilitate interactions between members of the community, external contributors and facilitators in order to develop a clear and consistent understanding of the purpose, mission, vision, and values of the community.
- *Changing participants*: community members, external contributors and facilitators will change over time. New participants will enter and existing participants will depart. The intent is to avoid a continuous turnover of the familiar.
- *Challenge*: once the community has established and documented its purpose, mission, vision and values, there must be a mechanism for challenge.
- *Personal development*: the infrastructure must enable individuals to assess their capacity to contribute to the effort, and provide a basis for personal development. This will enable individuals to develop their capacity to support the evolution of the leveragable body of knowledge.
- *Feedback*: community members interacting with the leveragable

body of knowledge must be able to provide feedback, and the feedback mechanism must be supported by the infrastructure.

• *Return on investment*: facilitators and external contributors must be able to reflect continually on their perceived return on investment from supporting the infrastructure. This provides a basis for determining whether alterations are appropriate to adjust the return on investment, and the facilitators' and external contributors' interactions with the system.

Wenger (1998) suggests that effective change processes consciously facilitate negotiation of meaning. In this model, negotiation consists of two interrelated components:

> If we believe that people in organisations contribute to organisational goals by participating inventively in practices that can never be fully captured by institutionalised processes. . . . we will have to value the work of community building and make sure that participants have access to the resources necessary to learn what they need to learn in order to take actions and make decisions that fully engage their own knowledgeability.
>
> (Wenger 1998:10)

The most effective school-to-school networks align individuals with a common, shared and clear set of objectives. They are also able to generate and create new knowledge that has a direct impact on the quality of learning in schools. As their central focus is *personalised learning*, the instructional benefits are always at the heart of any collaborative or networked activity. Co-construction ultimately defines and shapes the way they collaborate, share and generate new knowledge.

Hargreaves (2003:9) suggests that 'a network increases the pool of ideas on which any member can draw and that networks extend and enlarge the communities of practice with enormous potential benefits'. There is emerging evidence that school networks provide the spaces for knowledge creation, which impacts positively upon instructional processes. However, we need to know much more about the nature, processes and impact of school networks. We need to know whether they can be scaled up, if they are sustainable in the mid to long term, whether and how the networks connect to each other and the effect such *macro-communities* of practice might have on the system.

Distributed leadership and networks

The education systems of the future will undoubtedly be formed through *emergent partnerships* and *networks* of schools. It will be a system led *by schools for schools* demanding leadership that is widely distributed within and across schools. There will be four requirements of the 'new' leadership. It will need to:

- cross structural, cultural and political barriers;
- build capacity within schools, communities and systems;
- generate social capital;
- sustain performance through system self-renewal.

Collectively these four requirements present a considerable challenge to our schools and the leaders within them. They demand some serious thinking about what constitutes leadership and who leads, and more importantly they question conventional leadership solutions to contemporary leadership problems.

Hutchins (1995) emphasises the interdependence of the individual and highlights how human activity is widely distributed across a complex system. This work also emphasises the power of 'lateral agency', in other words, the potential for change and learning to emerge in a horizontal as well as a vertical direction.

> It is possible for a team to organize its behaviour in an appropriate sequence without there being a global script or plan anywhere in the system. Each crew member only needs to know what to do when certain conditions are produced in the environment.

Distributed leadership implies that the practice of leadership is one that is *shared* and realised within extended groupings and teams: some of these groupings will be formal while others will be informal and in some cases, randomly formed. Distributed leadership within networks can, at one level, be achieved by establishing new leadership roles such as lead learner, enquiry advocate, strand leader and programme leader. For example,

> A school in Hartlepool invited volunteer teachers to form collaborative enquiry groups to investigate questions generated by a network-wide audit of the 'barriers to learning'. Groups of teachers were given time and space to enquire together into an

aspect of their professional lives, developing an expertise to share within and across their schools.

One of the key characteristics of a distributed leadership is that space is created for leaders to learn from each other.

> In Pendle Small Schools Learning Community the classroom assistants who support children encountering difficulties with reading and writing have become the 'experts' in leading the network-wide dyslexia-friendly school programme, the key individuals working with those children, but also meeting to share, debate and develop the project.

Distributing leadership essentially means providing the opportunity and space to distribute learning across the network.

> Teachers meet in a termly 'learning forum'. This takes place after school, attendance is voluntary and attended by up to half of the school staff. This is a place where staff share what they have been learning form the study of their practice. The learning forum in Prudhoe is replicated across the network both within individual schools but also between schools. A place to share the successes they have had, the difficulties they have encountered and an invitation to the others present to help, to begin to answer the next questions that are emerging. A place where distributed leadership is enacted.

There is evidence that *school-to-school* networks are providing schools with an effective innovation system that allows schools to link, share, adapt and adopt new ideas. They are powerful platforms for the leverage of knowledge and the acceleration of innovation. This 'leveragable body of knowledge' is potentially important if the infrastructure of school networks is to fulfil its aim of producing and amplifying new knowledge. Nonaka and Takeuchi (1995) identify two sets of dynamics that drive the process of knowledge amplification:

- converting tacit into explicit knowledge;
- moving knowledge from the individual level to the group, organisational and inter-organisational levels.

The latter requires some form of knowledge leveraging that is very visible within the practices of school networks. This 'leveragable' body of knowledge is *all the knowledge available to the community* via all participants in the system. The repository for captured knowledge, the knowledge base, must provide feedback in support of its own continued development and evolution. It must also support the following types of interactions from each of the participants within the system.

Distributed leadership means that decision making, communication and direction are provided within and across school networks. It suggests that leadership is most effective in complex systems when it is *laterally distributed and shared*. This suggests that distributed leadership practice is a vehicle of knowledge transfer and knowledge creation. But what does distributed leadership look like? The next two chapters illuminate different forms of distributed leadership in practice.

Distributed leadership practice
Within schools

> There is a simpler way to lead organisations, one that requires less effort and produces less stress than our current practices.
>
> (Wheatley, 1999)

Introduction

Education reform is at a point where many of the ingredients of improvement are already in place in schools and school systems. The precise mix of processes may look different in different contexts but essentially the components are the same. Even though many reform efforts have contributed to improvement and in many cases have appeared to do the right thing, many more have fallen short and have failed to deliver lasting improvement (McKinsey, 2007). Part of the reason, as highlighted earlier, has been the over emphasis on prescription and external accountability as the main levers of change. Part of the reason also resides in the way our schools are currently organised. Structural resistance can be a powerful barrier to farreaching and deep improvement. The infrastructure of schools, by design or default, is currently proving to be a barrier to long-term transformation.

Inevitably there comes a time when radical change is needed to move the system forward. Fullan et al (2007:13) talk about a 'system stalled' and the need to *break through* the current system so that all students can achieve their potential. Michael Barber in his book *Instruction to Deliver* highlights that 'flogging a system that can no longer achieve certain goals' is pointless. He adds, 'reform is the key' (Barber, 2007: 193). While this is true, the nature and focus of the reform process is important. System reform is only possible if those within the education system, at all levels, subscribe to the changes and are actively engaged in system re-design (Hargreaves, 2007). System reform is only desirable if it is genuinely concerned with improving learning and the life chances of *all learners*.

The limitations of top–down reform are now well understood, and have been starkly documented (McKinsey, 2007). So what are the catalysts for future reform and how sure are we that they will secure improved learning and life chances? Zuboff and Maxim (2002:12) argue that existing organisational structures are able to stretch, adopt and adapt, but only so far. In order to move beyond existing practice to new, or even next practice, they suggest that organisations will have to:

> release lifeboats capable of charting a course into and through individual space and staking a claim there. The challenge for lifeboaters will be to define the coastline: the ways and means of establishing vital interdependencies with individuals in individual space. The crew will require a broad vision.

The central idea here is that sustainable educational transformation is unlikely to occur without some radical change in organisational structures. This is not to suggest that the current systems have little value or that they need to be instantly replaced. It is simply to ask whether our existing structures are fit for contemporary educational needs and purposes.

But changing structures alone will not bring system transformation. Re-arranging structures without some consideration of cultural change is unlikely to secure improvement. Changing structures without concomitant changes in culture and practices will result in cosmetic, superficial improvement and the inevitable *repetitive change syndrome* that can be distracting and draining. As Abrahamson (2004) notes:

> Not only do tidal shifts of change create pain at almost every level . . . they also impinge on routine operations and render forms inwardly focused on managing change rather than outwardly focused on customers these changes should serve.
>
> (Abrahamson, 2004:2–3).

There is certainly a danger that valuable time, resources and expertise will be wasted by restructuring without any real or clear focus on improving learning. However, it is also unlikely that any deep change in practice will occur without some form of structural change. Knowing which structures to replace or to remove is crucially important. 'Creative destruction' describes the process of transformation that accompanies radical innovation (Schumpeter, 1942). While the creative destruction of past ways of working is not always required or indeed desirable, it shouldn't automatically be discounted. Transformational change is a 'struggle to escape from habitual modes of thought and expression' (Keynes, 1936). It inevitably requires a separation from previous ways of working.

There are occasions when only a departure from old ways of operating will work and 'creative recombination' (i.e. the redeployment and recombination of existing elements in the system into new configurations) will not be the optimum way forward (Abrahamson, 2004). The challenge is to identify *exactly* what aspects of the organisation require change and to systematically and purposefully re-adjust, reconstruct and re-align organisational structures, so they can become more effective, which in schools means more able to support learning. Rather than randomly abandoning previous practices, dismantling structures for the sake of it or demolishing current ways of working, those schools that have successfully redefined and re-designed themselves have done so with the ultimate goal of improving learning outcomes.

So what does this have to do with distributed leadership? The argument in the remainder of the book is that distributed leadership encompasses both structural and cultural change. In other words, where schools have purposefully redesigned their structures, with the prime aim of extending and deepening leadership activity, there is more likely to be a positive impact on culture and a subsequent impact on learning. Without structural change, distributed leadership can occur, but the question is whether it is occurring in a way that supports learning. Without broader, deeper forms of leadership practice (see Chapter 9), the possibility of building professional learning communities is more remote.

As the following case studies show, structural changes that allow broad-based leadership to flourish have to be accompanied by a high degree of trust along with strong internal accountability processes. Simply distributing responsibility, without the associated accountability for decision-making, is unlikely to be effective and indeed, could be counterproductive.

The cases also illustrate that there is no single blueprint or model for effective distributed practice. As Spillane and Diamond (2007:150) point out, distributed leadership is not a 'prescription or a five-point plan'. While this is certainly true, the case studies reveal that there are some shared characteristics or features of distributed leadership in schools. These will be highlighted later. While structural change may be a common denominator across all the schools, the nature of distributed leadership practice varies considerably. Diversity rather than conformity is the norm.

This chapter provides examples of the ways schools have restructured to distribute leadership more widely. It will look at the different patterns of distributed leadership practice, and will focus on the relationship between changes in structures, culture and organisational outcomes. Before moving to these accounts of practice, it is important to first understand the broader context for organisational redesign in England, as this has been highly influential in guiding the re-structuring process in many schools.

Organisational redesign and workforce reform

In England, the demands of accountability plus the pressure of new initiatives designed to raise standards pushed schools to the brink. It soon became apparent that schools were bending, if not breaking under the sheer weight of external pressures and demands. There was an urgent need to address issues of workload and work-life balance within the teaching profession. In addressing this problem, the Government faced two choices: either to continue to push the system and schools to the very edge, and certain burnout, or to urgently reform school structures and work practices.

Extensive independent research undertaken on behalf of the Government in 2000 found that:

- workload was the major reason cited by teachers for leaving the profession;
- over 30 per cent of a teacher's working week was spent on non-teaching activities;
- teachers generally had a poor work/life balance;
- one in five newly qualified teachers were leaving the profession before they reached their fourth year of teaching;
- there were as many people in the general workforce trained as teachers but not working in the profession as there were teachers.

It was widely acknowledged that all of these factors were not only having a detrimental effect upon those remaining in the profession but also, as a consequence, pupil learning was inevitably suffering. The Government realised that if it did not introduce changes to teachers' conditions of service, matters would only worsen, especially as 45 per cent of the teaching workforce were due to retire within the next 15 years.

In October 2002 the Department for Education and Skills (DfES) published *Time for standards: reforming the school workforce*, which set out the Government's plans for creating additional time for teachers and head teachers and therefore time for raising educational standards (DfES, 2002). In January 2003, the Government, employers and trades unions (with the exception of the NUT) agreed to the principles of *Raising Standards and Tackling Workload: a National Agreement* (DfES, 2003). This agreement set out a seven-point plan, to be implemented over three years, to reduce teachers' workload and improve standards.

In 2004 the Children Act and the publication of *Every Child Matters: Change for Children* (DfES, 2004) defined the important relationship between educational well-being in childhood and later life. In June 2005 a prospectus for extended schools was published setting out the *core offer* of services that by 2010 would be accessible through schools, often beyond a school day, to help meet the needs of children, their families and the wider community (DfES, 2005).

A national analysis of teacher workload identified 24 tasks not directly related to teaching and learning, which were frequently carried out by teachers. Since September 2003 teachers have not been expected to undertake these tasks. From September 2004 there has been a limit on the amount of absence cover that a teacher can be asked to do and from September 2005 teachers would not be expected to invigilate examinations. This *Planning Preparation and Assessment* time (PPA) time is roughly equivalent to 10 per cent of their teaching timetable.

> The purpose of guaranteed PPA time is to enable teachers to raise standards through individual or collaborative professional activity. The contractual change on PPA is also designed to improve teachers' work/life balance.

The impact of 'Workforce Remodelling' has been significant for two reasons:

- firstly because it encouraged schools to undertake major *structural* changes that had previously been impossible to contemplate;
- secondly, because it encouraged schools to consider *alternative approaches to leadership*. This freedom to re-structure has allowed schools to think much more creatively about leadership practice and particularly, how leadership could be more closely aligned to learning and teaching processes.

A report by OfSTED (2007:6) noted that the workforce 'reforms had resulted in a revolutionary shift in workforce culture with clear benefits for many schools'. They also noted that the expansion of the wider workforce and an increasing breadth and diversity of roles were leading to changes in working practices at *all levels* in the schools.

The habitual mode of thought that teachers are best placed to undertake all the activities associated with teaching and learning in a school has vanished. The idea that leadership is only what the head or the senior leadership team do has also largely disappeared. In many schools support staff, parents, students and other professionals are now undertaking a wide range of leadership responsibilities.

'Workforce Reform' in England undoubtedly provided an important opportunity for schools to redesign their leadership structures. The resulting changes range from the radical redesign to tinkering at the edges. In some schools it provided the opportunity to extend leadership roles and leadership responsibilities. In other schools it simply consolidated and endorsed the leadership practices that were already in place.

Distributed leadership in practice

The following sets of cases provide illustrations of the ways in which some schools have redefined, realigned and revised their leadership structures with the prime purpose of improving learning and teaching. The cases illustrate how schools have deliberately created new patterns of leadership responsibility and provided new sources of leadership to support changes in instructional practices. The cases also offer an insight into the different ways schools have restructured to broaden leadership activity.

Across the cases there are some common principles that emerge about distributed leadership:

- it is *broad-based* leadership;

- it requires multiple levels of *involvement* in decision-making;
- it focuses primarily   on improving classroom *practice* or instruction;
- it encompasses both formal and *informal* leaders;
- it links vertical and lateral leadership structures;
- it extends to students and encourages *student voice*;
- it is *flexible* and versatile (non-permanent groupings);
- it is *fluid* and interchangeable;
- it is ultimately concerned with *improving* leadership practice in order to influence teaching and learning.

In Spillane's (2006) terms a distributed perspective implies that leadership is *stretched* over the work of multiple leaders. Using this perspective, Spillane and Diamond (2007) characterise different types of co-leading. The first type, 'collaborated distribution' is carried out by multiple leaders working together at one time and place. This could be an SLT meeting, departmental planning session or a learning mentor conference. The second type of distributed leadership is 'collective distribution', where leaders performing separately can nonetheless be interdependent. For example, assessment for learning may be a whole school priority but carried out in different ways by teachers and support staff. However, their work is interdependent.

The third form of distributed leadership highlighted by Spillane and Diamond (2007) is 'coordinated distribution'. This refers to the routines that are performed in a sequence. For example, leaders at different layers in the organisation will have access to progress data for year groups and individual children. They will use this data in different ways to track pupils, provide intensive intervention or look at progress against targets. However this core data and its use will be co-ordinated across the various users and at times, interpretation of the data will be used for more than one purpose. Spillane and Diamond (2007) would argue that the set of *routines and practices* around data interpretation, analysis and sharing offer a set of routines that constitute distributed leadership practice.

Their key argument here is that *multiple leaders* have expertise and knowledge that exceed what individual leaders possess or know – the sum of the parts is greater than the whole. Their main contention therefore is that group or collective interactions equate with *leadership practice*, not individual actions. Spillane and Diamond (2007) also note that these group interactions do not necessarily need to be harmonious or friendly.

School leaders don't have to see eye to eye or even get along with each other to co-perform leadership routines and tasks. Leadership can be stretched over leaders, even when they are not striving for the same ends. When leaders don't see eye to eye, they still work as a collective in co-performing a leadership routine. Whether two or more leaders seek similar, different, or even opposing goals is just another dimension of the analysis.

(Spillane and Diamond, 2007:31)

Here is an important point of departure between Spillane and Diamond's (2007) work and the idea of distributed leadership being explored in this book. Spillane and Diamond (2007) explore leadership functions as they impact particularly on instructional practices. Their interest is in describing and analysing key aspects of the tools, routines and situation outlined in their model of distributed leadership. Their examples examine how leadership practice shapes some of the key organisational routines and tools and how these in turn shape leadership practice.

The cases that follow offer insights into the way that schools have actively *re-structured* leadership roles and *redefined* leadership practices in order to impact positively upon teaching and learning. The emphasis is upon the *deliberate design* and construction of different patterns or configurations of formal and informal leadership roles within and between schools. The prime aim of the cases is to illuminate different approaches to leadership distribution and to highlight, where evidence is available, the difference leadership distribution has made to organisational and student learning outcomes.

A model of distributed leadership practice

The following model has been derived from empirical data collected from various studies focused, in part, on distributed leadership (Harris et al, 2007). The model outlines different types of leadership distribution *within, between and outside* schools. Some schools may have all three types of distribution and may have multiple levels of distributed leadership practice.

The purpose of this model is to represent the complexity and the possible variation of distributed leadership practice in schools. It aims to illuminate and illustrate the different forms and patterns of distributed leadership activity. The categorisation used in the model offers one way of delineating different forms of distributed leadership. There are no doubt others.

The model categorises distributed leadership in three ways:

- *Within schools*: restructuring roles and responsibilities, new teams, new responsibilities, teacher and student leadership.
- *Between schools*: collaborations, federations, networked activity.
- *Outside schools*: multi-agency, partnership, extended schools, schools as a social centre and community engagement.

The model is linked to the idea of system redesign (Hargreaves, 2007) outlined earlier in the book, which suggests that there is a need to build capacity within the system in order to transform it. To unleash transformational potential within the system will require new routes of influence, new innovation pathways, new knowledge and new patterns of leadership practice.

It is suggested that distributed leadership is the *organisational circuitry* that will ensure the fast flow of innovation and change. By creating more leadership opportunities and by increasing the surge of information between and across organisations, there is greater

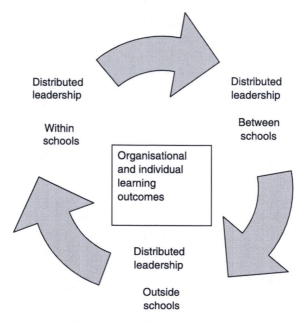

Figure 7.1 Model of distributed leadership.

potential for knowledge creation and system transformation. To successfully release potential within the system will require both lateral and vertical forms of leadership. The particular combination of lateral and vertical leadership will vary from context to context. The architecture of distribution will depend of the transformational needs of the school or system.

The cases that follow offer some insights into the way in which leadership has been deliberately orchestrated and re-modelled to generate opportunities for innovation and change. The scope and the scale of the distribution differ in each example but the core principle of *redesign* is central to all the cases and a common denominator in the process of raising achievement. As highlighted earlier many schools are engaged in *all three* forms of leadership distribution.

Distributed leadership within schools

Kanes Hill Primary School

Context

Kanes Hill is a primary school serving a socio-economically disadvantaged area in the suburbs of Southampton. The area, from which the school draws the majority of its pupils, consists largely of council-owned rented housing. Some private housing exists, largely properties bought by former council tenants under the 'right to buy' legislation. There are high levels of poverty on the estate and many single-parent families. The school is in the top 10 per cent most deprived areas in the country: 15.6 per cent of the children live in overcrowded houses and 32 per cent are on the Special Educational Needs Register.

In 1997 the school was identified as a school that was consistently and seriously under-performing. Since 1997 results have been improving and in 2004 it was identified as being in the top 1 per cent of contextual value[1] added. The majority of children start school far below the baseline in terms of literacy and numeracy. Many have poorly developed language and behavioural skills. The 2000 OfSTED

---

1 Contextual value added is the relative performance of the school given the starting point of the young people entering it.

inspection report[2] identified some weaknesses at the school, particularly in key stage 1.[3] In 2005, the OfSTED report highlighted that both the school and the leadership were considered to be *excellent*. The school was named as one of the most outstanding schools by inspectors. Since that time, the school has remained consistently in the top quartile for value added over the past four years, and was in the top 2 per cent in 2007.

Distributed leadership

In 2000, the deputy head became the acting head teacher, and was subsequently appointed as the permanent head. It was clear that major change was needed within the school and that there had to be a significant shift in expectations of achievement. The first year was spent establishing new ways of working, higher expectations and embedding consistent approaches to teaching and learning. In 2000 the school produced a strategic intent document, which summarised the main areas for development over the next two years.

The head was keen to develop a culture of shared understanding, shared responsibility and shared accountability among all staff at the school. She believed that everyone in the school was a potential leader and she was committed to distributing leadership widely. There was a recognition that the scale of the improvement task could not be undertaken by the senior leadership team alone and therefore one of the stated strategic intents was to 'build leadership depth throughout the school'. The actions for achieving this were clearly outlined in the strategic intent document (2000–2002):

1   Support the staff to take on responsibility to deal with issues as they arise.
2   Provide leadership and management development for *all* staff.
3   Develop a no blame culture where staff are encouraged to take risks.
4   Provide a forum for staff to discuss their roles in an ever-changing environment.
5   Develop a culture of sharing expertise.

2   OfSTED (2000). The Office for Standards in Education (OfSTED) is a national body and inspects schools on a regular cycle.
3   Key stage 1 covers ages 5–7.

In the strategic document 2004–2007 this was further refined to include:

- promote *leadership at every level*, including pupils;
- develop reflective practice;
- encourage staff to innovate and take risks;
- continue to support staff to take on responsibility and to deal effectively with issues as they arise.

For many staff in the school, the new approach to leadership involved a considerable 'leap of faith'. The previous leadership had mainly restricted decision-making to the head and deputy head. Now an extended senior leadership team plus year teams, a Special Educational Needs (SEN) team and support-staff teams are all involved in decision-making. The head invested time and a great deal of support in establishing effective team working among staff. The tightly defined strategic intent meant that staff could take risks and make decisions but within the parameters agreed to take the school forward.

Gradually, individuals took on more responsibility at the school, and the constant drive for consistency of teaching and learning began to impact upon pupil performance. The teaching assistants are now fully involved in supporting the decision-making process and there is a student council that meets with the Senior Leadership Team (SLT). There is a strong team spirit at the school and all staff are included in professional development and training. The school has also recently embarked upon developmental work and is currently working on developing a more creative curriculum.

Commentary

The head believes that distributing leadership at the school has played a major part in the school's transformation. She is currently on secondment and her deputy is the acting head teacher, so the systems set in place are running very effectively without her presence. She feels that this is the 'acid test' of distributed leadership, i.e. the school is not overly dependent on the formal leader being there every day. Her view is that distributing leadership widely within the school has ensured that *the school continues to thrive and maintain its high standards of performance*.

The model of distributed leadership at the school is strongly based on team working and team support within a very clear vision and strategic intent. Staff are highly motivated at the school, and see themselves as being able to take responsibility for making decisions. There is also a strong accountability structure, through performance management, so all staff are aware that they are both responsible and accountable for actions and decisions taken. Distributed leadership has been carefully and purposefully orchestrated by the head. This is considered to be one of the reasons why the school continues to be an outstanding school in exceptionally challenging circumstances.

John Cabot Academy[4]

Context

John Cabot Academy is a school serving Bristol, and is situated in Kingswood in the North East of the City.

Originally a City Technology College,[5] it opened its doors for the first time in September 1993 and enrolled 160 Bristol students aged 11. The design capacity of this purpose-built secondary school is around 1,000, and it caters for students aged 11–18 years.

John Cabot CTC was one of the first 15 schools in a programme that led to the development of well over 2,000[6] specialist schools in England. In 2007 John Cabot became an Academy. It works closely with business and industry, particularly through its sponsors,

4 Academies are publicly funded independent schools, with the freedom to raise standards through innovative approaches to management, governance, teaching and curriculum. They are established in disadvantaged areas, either as new schools, or to replace poorly performing schools, where other intervention and improvement strategies have failed. Academies are established by sponsors from the business, faith and voluntary sectors who contribute up to £2 million towards the capital costs of the new building.

5 City Technology Colleges are funded directly by the government and offer a wide range of vocational qualifications alongside A-levels or equivalents. They teach the National Curriculum with a specific focus on science, mathematics and technology. Most CTCs teach a longer day and several operate a five-term year. CTCs have developed close links with employers. They are technically independent schools.

6 See www.ssat.org for further information. Any maintained secondary school in England may apply to be designated as a specialist school in one of ten specialisations. Schools can also combine any two specialisations. These are as follows: arts (performing, visual or media) business and enterprise engineering, humanities, language, mathematics and computing, music, science, sports, technology.

the Wolfson Foundation and Rolls Royce PLC. Representatives from these companies, and others, advise and support the Academy in all aspects of its running, and also sit on its governing body.

The Academy is designed for a maximum of 156 students per year group in Years 7–11, along with a sixth form of 240. John Cabot is working in a federation with the newly established Bristol Brunel Academy (BBA). John Cabot Academy is the educational sponsor of BBA, with David Carter acting as Executive Principal, having overall responsibility for both academies. Both academies have their own principals who have the day-to-day responsibility for the schools.

John Cabot is a high performing school, as confirmed by the 2007 OfSTED inspection where it was judged to be 'outstanding'. When the principal was appointed in 2004, 63 per cent of its students achieved five GCSEs (A–C).[7] In subsequent years this has increased from 71 per cent to 75 per cent and by a further 8 per cent to 83 per cent in 2007. This constitutes a 20 per cent improvement over three academic years. 73 per cent of students at the college achieved five A*–C grades including English and maths in 2007.

The Academy acknowledges that a range of strategies have helped them to improve their results. These have included curriculum development, mentoring, ICT developments and the rigorous monitoring of student performance. The school has also used the workforce reform dynamically to impact upon student learning. Many support staff are also tutors and mentors. The principal notes that

> the people who've got a leadership role in the school now are really focused upon teaching and learning ... that wasn't the case when I came, there were lots of people doing jobs around the periphery of teaching and learning but they weren't directly engaged in it or chose not to be.

Distributed leadership

The John Cabot Academy deliberately restructured in order to move away from a staff composition that was largely separated into teachers and support staff, to becoming a team of adults working

---

7 GCSEs are the examination at 16; grades A–C are the benchmark for gauging a school's performance.

towards developing the learning of all young people. It created new roles and appointed people from outside education to come in and undertake strategic leadership roles.

A team of cover supervisors[8] was set up, and a curriculum administrator was appointed to take care of exams, cover and staff training. The staffing composition changed from 70 per cent per cent teaching staff and 30 per cent support staff to closer to a 65/35 split.

The pastoral model that the current principal inherited was the traditional 'head of year' model. This has been changed and there are now two adults in every tutor group with tutor groups of 13 or 14, one is a lead tutor and one acts as a link tutor. Every single member of the teaching staff, including the principal, is a tutor. There are also 10 members of support staff who provide additional capacity. Every tutor is also a mentor, and the children are mentored once every seven weeks.

The principal also put in place a system where 'gap year' students stay with the Academy for a year after their A levels.[9] They are paid a bursary for a year on the condition that they are interested in becoming a teacher. The intention is that some may return on the 'Graduate Teacher Programme'[10] after they have completed their degree.

In addition to broadening roles and building capacity the Academy also operates a flatter leadership structure. As the principal notes:

> Leadership, I would say here, is a much flatter structure than in any other school I've ever been responsible for or worked in. There's a leadership team which is a strategic group and then there's an extended leadership team of about 7 or 8 people who are charged with the operational day to day running of the school. People who are now in senior leadership posts have a very clear remit around performance and teaching and learning.

At John Cabot Academy, the principal has deliberately tried to distribute leadership authority and responsibility. The Academy has been restructured into five schools, and each assistant principal runs a mini school. The assistant principals are directly responsible to the

8 When a teacher is absent, 'cover' for the lesson is undertaken by a cover supervisor.
9 A Head of Year would have pastoral responsibility for an entire year group.
10 This consists of teacher training and entry for graduates.

principal and are accountable for the performance of their school. Within their school they have a great deal of latitude and flexibility to run things the way they choose, but ultimately they are accountable for student performance.

Comment

The impact of distributing leadership more widely at the school has been positively received. Support staff now feel empowered to undertake specific leadership roles. There is also a greater sense of risk-taking and innovation. As the principal notes:

> I think the culture is a very positive one, I think it's a 'can do' culture . . . we've got a very optimistic staff room, people are very creative, they take on new projects . . . willing to take risks, and are willing to engage in dialogue about innovation.

CourtFields Community School

Context

CourtFields Community School is a rural, 11–16, mixed comprehensive situated in Wellington, Somerset with 880 students. The school's intake at key stage 2^{11} is below national averages in all core areas. It is judged to be, in terms of intake, currently eighth lowest (out of 33 secondary schools). Over the last five years the results at the school have consistently improved. In 1999, the school achieved 53 per cent A–C grades, and has steadily increased attainment levels to 64 per cent in 2007.

The school has consistently performed above the national average. The school does not have a sixth form but on average 84 per cent of pupils go on to further education. The head was appointed at the school six years ago and in that time the school has been engaged in significant restructuring since and workforce remodelling aimed at distributing leadership more widely and improving achievement levels. The school has doubled its support staff in the past six years.

The leadership team was restructured to include the head, and a new deputy plus three new assistant head posts. In the past the senior

11 Aged 11.

leadership team (SLT) consisted of the head and two deputies. Each member of the newly formed SLT is also responsible for a year group, and has specific teaching and learning responsibilities. For example, one assistant head is responsible for leading intervention work with year 7,[12] which has made a significant difference to increasing the attainment of level 4 in English and Maths.

In addition, there are associate members of the senior leadership team (SLT) who volunteer to serve for a two-year period. There is no remuneration for taking on this additional responsibility, and after two years the opportunity is extended to other members of staff. This way the leadership team is continually refreshed and reformulated, and potential leaders in the organisation have direct experience of working in the SLT. It also ensures that the leadership team connects with different parts of the organisation and keeps a relentless focus on teaching and learning.

Distributed leadership

The school has distributed leadership widely through the extensive use of support staff, particularly teaching assistants. It has also created new posts aimed at supporting teaching and learning processes across the school. In the past few years the school has appointed a number of Higher Level Teaching Assistants (HLTAs).

In a previous OfSTED inspection CourtFields was judged to be a 'very inclusive' school, but it was recognised that the school had a number of very challenging students. The curriculum did not always meet the needs of these students and, in some cases, they were not able to access learning because of emotional difficulties. It was clear that staff were becoming worn down by the behaviour of a minority of students. Consequently, the school appointed a part-time HLTA who works one day a week to support students who have completed the year 7 programme, but need further confidence and support as they move into years 8 and 9.

One of the HLTAs runs the 'Student Support Centre', which focuses on behaviour and offers intervention to students who are unable to operate for a period of time in ordinary lessons. The Centre offers an alternative curriculum at KS4 and practical opportunities, extended work experience and an 'emotional curriculum', e.g. dealing with conflict, group skills and building self-esteem. Although

12   Year 7, students aged 11.

only established two years ago, there is evidence that the Centre has been effective in preventing exclusions and has been successful in re-integrating pupils back into mainstream teaching.

All the HLTAs work independently but are supported by staff in a technologically rich learning environment. They have dedicated classroom space and work in close collaboration with teaching staff. Most students work with HLTAs for a period of time and then return to their original class. In extreme cases some students have a personalised learning programme in the Student Support Centre.

There is a strong emphasis on continuous professional development for all staff, coaching is well embedded and has recently been extended to include support staff. The school has recently achieved the 'Investors in People' award for the fourth time. The support staff and teaching staff structures intertwine and there is a strong sense of collaboration and collegiality. All teaching and support staff are professional mentors and there is considerable role crossover.

In addition, there is a strong emphasis on student leadership. Students have their own council which includes a small budget with clear lines into formal decision-making processes. They are always involved in all interviews and lead on developmental priorities with the school such as environmental issues. They lead staff training sessions particularly, on assessment for learning, and there is a system of student mentoring and support.

Throughout the school there are many points of influence and decision-making. Leadership comes from different directions and who leads depends upon the issue or the problem that the school is facing or tackling. The leadership team is receptive and open to new ideas and challenges. The formal and informal leadership roles intersect around teaching and learning issues. The collective purpose is one of raising achievement and ensuring high levels of care for all students. The head is clear that in the future the configuration of leadership practice and processes will alter to suit the changing needs of the school. Her aim has been to produce a flexible leadership structure that combines informal and formal roles within the school.

The main outcomes from distributing leadership across support and teaching staff have been a significant rise in the percentage of students converting level 3 entry to level 5+ at the end of KS3 and achieving a C grade at the end of KS4 in Maths and English. In

English the school is now in the top group of the Fisher Family Trust, while in Maths the school is in the top group for KS3 and second group for KS4.

Students also report significant improvement in their own skills and confidence. Targeted students in Science and DT have shown marked improvements in grades. Coursework marks have risen significantly. With students in the Student Support Centre there has been a reduction in fixed-term exclusion and the avoidance of permanent exclusions. There is considerable evidence that students enjoy the more practical, vocational programmes offered.

Commentary

In the past six years the school has dramatically increased its support staff, diversified its leadership roles and created new leadership posts. The leadership structure is widely distributed and the culture is now one where there is an interchange of roles and responsibilities. The form of distribution has been structured around improving teaching and learning. There is evidence that the distributed leadership structure is having a positive impact upon levels of attainment and achievement at the school as improved performance levels have been sustained over a five-year period.

Weobley High School

Context

Weobley High School in Hereford is an 11–16 mixed comprehensive school maintained by the Herefordshire Local Education Authority. The number of pupils on roll is approximately 446. In May 2004, the school was placed in Special Measures. In December 2005 the school was removed from this category completely. No notice to improve was deemed necessary. Results have increased from 41 per cent, in 2004 to 55 per cent in 2005 and 68 per cent in 2006. In the spring of 2006 the school was awarded Specialist Language status.

There have been many changes undertaken at the school to raise its performance, including a more distributed model of decision-making:

- Staff had to 'buy into' the philosophy that students came first in every aspect of decision making.

- Each member of the staff team was equally important in fulfilling their function in the school; this included all teachers and support staff.
- The most vital 'tool' for success was considered to be the engendering of positive relationships between student and student, staff members and students, staff members with each other, and most importantly the positive three-way partnership between staff, student and home.
- Communication was improved at all levels, and developments in the area of student and parent voice were seen as a major component of the change agenda.
- A new staffing structure became the driving force behind redesigning learning support at all levels, and giving more status to associate staff.

Distributed leadership

Across the school significant changes were made in staffing roles and responsibilities in order to extend leadership and to locate it closer to teaching and learning. The senior leadership team was reduced to a head teacher and two deputies. An assistant head post was removed in order to create a non-teaching curriculum support manager who became an associate member of the SLT.

- Heads of year were changed into learning co-ordinators with a prime focus on achievement and a responsibility for shared target setting with students, tracking, intervention and parental links.
- The finance officer role changed to a more significant role of school business manager, co-ordinating business development work.
- An office manager post was created to bring coherence to home/ school links, high school/primary school links and to support the improvement of communication.

Two cover supervisors were appointed to support teaching and learning in a multitude of ways, including lesson cover for absent colleagues, cover for non-teaching staff absence, and small group withdrawal work.

- Administrative posts were linked to specific areas of student support and achievement. These posts relate to the senior leadership team.

- Effective and innovative use of talented teaching assistants was implemented to teach small groups (e.g. extra Literacy and Numeracy to the Key Stage 3+ group, Life Skills sessions).
- A 'work related' co-ordinator was appointed to a non-teaching post, to support career development for all students in the school, support work experience and enterprise education.

Commentary

At the school, leadership roles have changed and leadership practice has been extended. As a result there is evidence that teaching and learning at the school has improved. The curriculum on offer is more relevant and the school experience is more enjoyable and enriching for students and staff. The improved results have been achieved through a greater personalisation of learning opportunities, more associate staff supporting the full range of student needs, more adults other than teachers engaging with learners and leadership that is closer to the classroom.

It is the head teacher's view that distributing leadership more widely has resulted in increased achievement and standards at the school. The head feels that the reconfiguration of roles at the school was the catalyst for a whole series of changes that have altered the school culture and raised expectations. The school is already focused on creating learning opportunities outside the classroom, and is planning a more rich provision for 14–19 learning. It is possible that such changes will require a further realignment of leadership responsibilities in the future, but the current structure is flexible enough to adopt and adapt to new opportunities.

Tudor Grange School

Tudor Grange School is an 11–16 specialist technology college. In 2002, 83.4 per cent of the students achieved five A–C grades, and 68.3 per cent achieved five A–C grades including Maths and English. In 2007 the 97.3 per cent of the students achieved five A–C grades, 80 per cent of them including Maths and English. The head notes that the context is one 'where you have to keep moving forward, you can't afford to drop your performance and therefore risks, significant changes in anything are always a gamble'.

During the year 2005/2006, the school changed its staffing structure from a traditional hierarchical leadership models to a more distributed structure. The leadership structure in the school had been quite traditional with a head, two deputies, two assistant heads and heads of year.

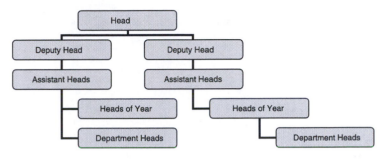

Figure 7.2 Traditional leadership model.

The school used the opportunity of teaching and learning responsibility points (TLRs) and staffing structure to rethink how it was organised. The school established five colleges (see Fig. 7.3).

The new college structure gave the school an opportunity to create teams, not just of teachers, but of associate staff, classroom supervisors, and learning mentors. There is an administrative team for each college which is a point of contact for students, parents, and teachers.

The main reasons for the re-structuring were:

- to create specialist support teams across the school;
- to improve academic mentoring and guidance;
- to create administrative support for every teaching and learning team;
- the leadership to focus on teaching and learning and standards of achievement;
- to create teaching and learning teams under one line management structure.

Each college is led by a member of the leadership team. Not all members necessarily have additional whole school strategic responsibilities to the college leader role. All colleges are supported by the Specialist Achievement Support team – this team deals with extreme cases of underachievement/learning difficulty where coordination of

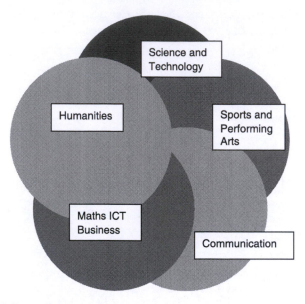

Figure 7.3 Five colleges.

external support agencies is required. All colleges are supported by the Achievement Support Team.

> As one college leader noted, 'I have to work through my team and the leadership group has to be a very empowered team, I've distributed responsibility, they are very accountable and really, to manage the whole thing and get it to work effectively, that has to be the way it operates.'

One of the challenges of operating as five separate colleges is one of consistency, and the teams spend a lot of time talking about procedures, systems, structures and implementation. The Lead Teacher (Achievement) in each college is also pivotal in securing consistency of teaching and learning. This post is responsible for the overall academic achievement of pupils in the college.

The Lead Teacher (Achievement) maintains effective tracking systems to identify underachievement in students of all abilities, coaches and mentors staff in the application of appropriate strategies to ensure pupils achieve their full potential. They also ensure that all pupils participate in at least one enrichment activity in each academic year and establish the essential routines, skills and knowledge for future academic success (learning to learn).

In addition the school has established a mentoring programme for pupils who are in danger of not achieving five A*–C grades. The outcomes of the Mentoring Programme have been very positive. In 2005, 26 pupils were supported and 65.4 per cent achieved five A*–C grades. In 2007, 49 pupils were supported, and 87.8 per cent achieved five A*–C grades. As one teacher noted,

> mentors working very closely with the teaching staff, beginning to understand exactly what it is the students have to do in order to get course work completed, looking at exam papers, understanding criteria and so on that has really, we feel, made such a significant difference.

Commentary

Tudor Grange School has moved from a very traditional leadership structure to a more distributed leadership model organised around five colleges with various support teams (achievement, mentoring, community, lead teacher and central services). The staff at the school feel that these changes have been beneficial and that the flatter, broader leadership structure has positively impacted on students' learning. As one teacher highlighted,

> the students are getting a better service than they were, because we are able to meet their needs more appropriately now and we couldn't have done that without making these changes to the leadership structure.

Another teacher comments that distributing leadership more widely has had:

> . . . a massive impact on how we work, we were clearly successful before but using the associate staff in a proactive way with the students there's no doubt we've been able to target the students and narrowed down the number of students who are not able to perform within the system. The biggest impact it has had is on the level of support we are able to supply to the youngsters and that clearly is recognised in terms of our GCSE outcomes.

In 2002 the school had 28 associate staff; it now has 44. In the future the school aims to expand the use of associate staff and to trial various teaching and learning models. The school also intends to explore the more imaginative uses of ICT and is currently looking at personalised staff development for all staff via an e-portfolio.

Northfleet Technology College

Context

Northfleet Technology College (NTC) is a boys' secondary modern school in Kent. As a local authority Kent has retained almost a quarter of the grammar schools in England and is therefore highly selective. As a consequence, 50 per cent of NTC students have special educational needs and many arrive at the school with very low prior attainment. In 1997 11 per cent of the students were achieving more than five A*–C grades, and it was clear that raising achievement had to be a key priority. OfSTED reports during the 1990s indicated that, while the educational provision was good, there was a clear need for improvement and raising standards. The school achieved specialist status as a technology college in 2003 and was re-designated in 2007.

The head has been in post since 1985. Although exam results were improving year-on-year, the head was concerned that a 'ceiling' was being reached, specifically at five A*–C grades at GCSE level, and that the leadership structure had to be fundamentally transformed if the school was to achieve the radical breakthrough in exam results.

The previous leadership structure incorporated a strong middle management structure with 14 heads of department. All the heads of department felt under enormous pressure to raise standards, and felt directly accountable for the performance of their subject area. Many heads of department were stressed by the degree of scrutiny and the extent of the responsibility for their department's performance. In particular, the heads of English, Maths and Science felt a disproportionate pressure on their subject areas to improve.

The head felt that the culture was ready for a new leadership structure, and actively sought to distribute leadership within the school. The need to raise standards, together with the advent of workforce remodelling, provided the opportunity to change the leadership structure radically. There were a number of reasons for this re-structuring:

- the need to create additional learning capacity: e.g. the percentage of five A*–C grades at GCSE needed to improve more rapidly;
- the need to embed distributed leadership at *all* levels – to build leadership capacity;
- staff had been working flat out – every strategy was exhausted;
- Head of Department accountabilities were becoming overwhelming, so leadership needed to be shared out.

Distributed leadership

Following an 18-month period of consultation and planning, in September 2006 the Head of Department role was disbanded and five new 'Learning Sets' were established (see Fig. 7.4):

- English, Music, Drama, Media, Film;
- Maths, History;
- Science, Geography, RE;
- Design and Technology, PE, Art;
- ICT, Business, modern foreign languages (MFL).

Each of the five 'learning sets' contains four leadership posts (incorporating key elements of the former head of department's role):

- Learning Programme Director;
- Lead Practitioner;
- Progress Manager;
- ICT Co-ordinator.

Additionally, the school appointed whole-school co-ordinators, working across the 'learning sets', including Literacy and Numeracy and Gifted and Talented.

The school has no Heads of Department, Heads of Subject or Heads of Year in the leadership structure. The job description of a form tutor and subject teacher includes aspects of these former roles, and it is assumed that as teachers move up the pay scale they will take on more responsibility at subject level.

The Learning Programme Director (LPD) is responsible for setting up systems to monitor progress of all students and staff, the management of learning set resources, including deployment of learning set

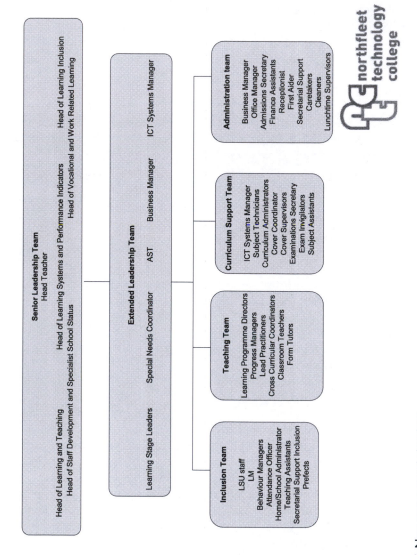

Senior Leadership Team
Head Teacher

Head of Learning and Teaching   Head of Learning Systems and Performance Indicators   Head of Learning Inclusion
Head of Staff Development and Specialist School Status   Head of Vocational and Work Related Learning

Extended Leadership Team

Special Needs Coordinator   AST   Business Manager   ICT Systems Manager

Learning Stage Leaders

Inclusion Team

LSU staff
LM
Behaviour Managers
Attendance Officer
Home/School Administrator
Teaching Assistants
Secretarial Support Inclusion
Prefects

Teaching Team

Learning Programme Directors
Progress Managers
Lead Practitioners
Cross Curricular Coordinators
Classroom Teachers
Form Tutors

Curriculum Support Team

ICT Systems Manager
Subject Technicians
Curriculum Administrators
Cover Coordinator
Cover Supervisors
Examinations Secretary
Exam Invigilators
Subject Assistants

Administration team

Business Manager
Office Manager
Admissions Secretary
Finance Assistants
Receptionist
First Aider
Secretarial Support
Caretakers
Cleaners
Lunchtime Supervisors

northfleet
technology
college

Figure 7.4 New management structure.

Source: School Prospectus, 2006.

assistants, ensuring an appropriate curriculum is delivered which meets national guidelines and the needs of the students.

The Lead Practitioner (LP) is a skilled teacher responsible for developing teaching and learning across the learning set. Teachers within each learning set, therefore, have access to 'their own' qualified advanced skills teacher (AST), or a teacher capable of fulfilling this role.

The Progress Manager (PM) is responsible for overseeing the progress of students across the learning set. This involves analysing and disseminating students' progress data, to ensure lessons are properly differentiated and that students are on track to meet their targets.

The ICT Co-ordinator (in this specialist Technology College) is responsible for:

- developing the use of ICT as a teaching and learning tool across the learning set;
- supporting the LPDs to develop an online curriculum;
- ensuring that ICT is delivered and assessed as a cross-curricular subject;
- representing the Learning Set on the ICT working party.

As noted above, the cross-curricular roles in each learning set are intended to support a number of areas, e.g. 'gifted and talented' education, literacy and PSHE.

There are also new support staff roles, including:

- behaviour managers;
- behaviour administration assistants;
- Community and Business Links Co-ordinator;
- Learning Set Assistants (including Cover Supervisors).

Leadership responsibility was distributed to those who had the ability plus the capacity to lead – *not those who necessarily had the subject expertise*. For example, the head of one Learning Set is a former Head of PE while another is a former Head of Music. They are both leading a wide range of other subjects within their learning set. Leadership responsibility has been given to those with the aspiration to lead rather than as so often happens, by default, to those with the most relevant subject expertise.

The new structure has also created four Learning Stage Leaders who are responsible for the curriculum organisation for identified year groups and ensuring all students in their stage are supported, enabling them to progress in a learning environment best suited to their needs. The Learning Stage Leaders manage a Learning Programme Director and form tutors.

All Learning Stage Leaders are on the Extended Leadership Team and are paid on the leadership scale. Some take on additional whole school responsibility and are also Assistant Heads. The school's five Learning Communities were also introduced in September 2006, and incorporate a vertical tutoring system encouraging distributed leadership within the form groups. Each of the new roles have been linked to performance management – while there is greater distribution of autonomy there is also more distribution of accountability.

Commentary

In 2006 the school was inspected and the OfSTED report highlighted that *leadership in the school was good*. In 2007, after just a year's implementation of its new structure, NTC gained its best ever KS3, Ks4 and post-16 exam results. As well as being in the top 1 per cent of schools nationally for KS2–3 attainment the school achieved 43 per cent A–C with English and Maths and the top 5 per cent nationally for KS4 Mathematics (CVA), the school achieved 43 per cent five A–C grades, and 94 per cent achieved A*–G with English and Maths. The school firmly believes that distributed leadership has provided the platform for transformation and has contributed to the significant improvement in results.

St Benedict's School, Derby

Context

St Benedict Catholic School and Performing Arts College is a larger than average secondary school in Derby. The percentage of students eligible for free school meals is in line with the national average and the proportion of students from ethnic minority backgrounds is higher than average. Students enter the school with expected levels of attainment. The percentage of students with statements of special educational needs is high but the proportion of students with learning difficulties and disabilities is average. Over half of the school's students continue their education in the sixth form.

Standards have improved steadily over recent years. Since 2003 the GCSE results have risen from 62 per cent in 2003 to 70 per cent in 2007. National standards at the end of Key Stage 3 national tests have also risen in Mathematics and Science. Contextual added value is close to the average. The school draws on a wide catchment area, which includes the inner city and some deprived areas. It has a very diverse and multi-ethnic student community and is particularly committed to the inclusion of students with physical disabilities and special needs.

The school currently has 107 teachers and 230 associate staff supported by a senior leadership team. In 2003 the head set up a 'remodelling workforce reform party', with the specific aim of re-structuring roles, including leadership roles, within the school. In the 18 months that followed a process of consultation with staff, governors and union representatives was undertaken. In June 2005 the new structure was implemented. It gave non-teaching staff leadership and line management responsibilities along with clear leadership roles.

Distributed leadership

The head saw workforce remodelling as an opportunity to re-think radically the leadership structures and practices within the school. The school had been awarded 'Investor in People'[13] status for the first time and had been commended for its strong teams. This was a further catalyst to creating a more distributed structure that allowed teams of teaching and associate staff to work together more effectively.

The first major change was to rename 'non-teaching staff' as associate staff, to eradicate any perceived differences in status. The restructuring and reallocation of leadership responsibilities and tasks was dependent on all staff playing a part, not just those with formal leadership titles. The hierarchical model of leadership was replaced with one that set out clear areas of responsibility for leaders in both teaching and associate roles. The current structure is shown in Fig. 7.5.

In addition, three new teams of associate staff were created, led by the Director of Administration, Director of Personnel and Director of Business and Development. The Directors are part of the Leadership team and have responsibility for a wide range of associate staff in the school. As members of the senior leadership team they play an

13 'Investors in People' is the national standard that sets out a level of good
    practice for the training and development of people in order to achieve business
    goals.

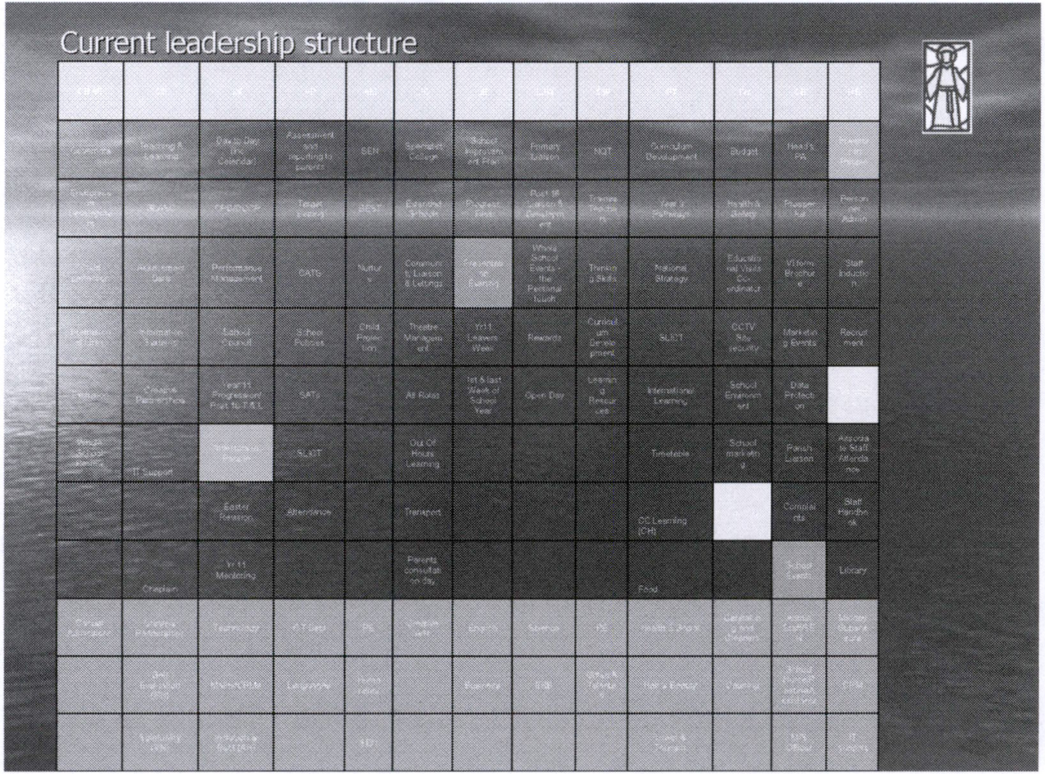

Figure 7.5 Current leadership structure.

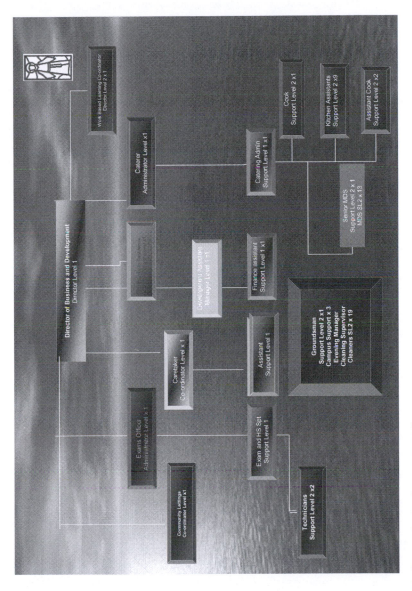

Figure 7.6 Current leadership structure II.

Source: School Prospectus, 2005.

equal role in setting the strategic direction and priorities for the school. They also have responsibility for their own teams and can make decisions and have a degree of autonomy within their areas of responsibility.

The new distributed leadership structure cannot be represented in one simple organisational chart. The connections and responsibilities are complex, crossing lateral and vertical boundaries, plus there are two-way connections between and across various teams.

The main challenge in the implementation of the new structure was attitudinal, as staff were used to a very different way of working and lacked confidence in their own leadership abilities. Also the new structure necessitated a high degree of trust to make it work. The distributed nature of the leadership inevitably meant that decisions were made on a daily basis without the endorsement of the head or senior leadership team. However, the establishment of a leadership forum within the school, involving anyone with a leadership responsibility, ensured that major decisions were always debated and agreed by a school-wide group.

Although the leadership forum is a large body, it has established clear ways of working with the smaller leadership team that provides strategic direction and advice. In 2007, 'Investors in People' was awarded to the school once again and the report noted that 'there is a really clear vision which is shared with and understood by staff at all levels. There is a motivated and skilled workforce where all employees have an opportunity to develop and lead'.

Commentary

The school has set up structures that involve more staff in decision-making. There are currently 12 consultation teams within the school, which comprise a cross-section of teaching and associate staff. These meet five times a year to look at particular issues the school is facing. The consultation groups were instrumental in moving the school towards a house system that the Head, personally, was not in favour of implementing. However the majority of staff felt that this would be a positive move and it was introduced two years ago.

The last OfSTED inspection undertaken in November 2006 noted that:

> The leadership of the school is good. There are some excellent features, particularly in the way responsibility is delegated, and

distributed, throughout the school, which enables the professionalism of its leaders to flourish. This has led to some initiatives of high quality, for example, the development of the house system. There is a positive culture of looking forward, a commitment to improvement, and an expectation that ideas will be listened to and taken seriously.

Overview

The examples of distributed leadership outlined in the school cases reflect diverse and different approaches to changing leadership practice. In some cases external opportunities to restructure were the catalyst for change. For other schools, it was the recognition that existing leadership structures were actively preventing the school from developing and improving.

Each of the schools has taken risks in order to secure radical change. The process of changing structures involves changing job descriptions, roles, status, expectations and inevitably leadership responsibilities. This is not easy but with consultation, discussion and debate it is possible. What is most important is that the head and the senior leadership team relinquish some responsibility and authority for decision-making within a clear framework of accountability. As one head noted,

> 'there cannot be distributed leadership without distributed followership; if people have the authority to make decisions, they are also accountable for them'.

There is no guarantee that leadership restructuring will work. Alongside restructuring has to be the process of re-culturing, where collaboration, trust and responsibility are nurtured, tested, reinforced and deeply embedded. Simply changing structures is not enough; it is cultural change that ultimately changes practices in schools and impacts on learning. But without some shift, breakthrough or rearrangement of structural alignment or responsibility it is unlikely that any major cultural change will occur. If it does, it is likely to be unsustainable in the long term.

It is clear from the emerging research base that patterns or configurations of distributed leadership vary from school to school. The evidence shows that some patterns are more effective than others in terms of promoting organisational and individual learning

(Leithwood et al, 2007). Where distributed leadership seems to be making a difference to organisational outcomes and performance, it is also where schools have deliberately and purposefully redesigned leadership in order to meet *their* particular needs or challenges. They have not simply borrowed structures from other schools but have adopted, adapted and reformulated leadership practices to suit their school context.

The next chapter focuses on schools that are distributing leadership between schools, through partnerships, networks and federations. It also looks at distributed leadership outside schools, where schools are sharing leadership responsibility with other agencies and organisations.

Chapter 8

Distributed leadership practice

Between and outside schools

Introduction

In the past, schools tended to work in relative isolation with relatively few links to other schools or organisations. While this way of working might have been appropriate a decade or so ago, there is now increased pressure on schools to establish partnerships with other schools, agencies and professionals.

Senge (1990; et al, 1994) suggests that networks of schools offer the possibility of new ways of working. He emphasises collaborative learning and team skills as being the key to successful and sustainable organisational development, rather than an adherence to individual skills and individual learning. His work has shown the potential for redesigning local systems and structures by promoting different forms of collaboration, linkages and multi-functional partnerships (Senge et al, 2005). In England and in other countries, school networks are increasingly being seen as a means of generating innovation and change as well as contributing to large-scale system reform (Hopkins, 2001; OECD, 2005).

Collaboration remains central to the 'Transforming Secondary Education' agenda in England. Within this agenda, diversity and collaboration are the two main driving forces for raising standards. In particular, federations of schools are viewed as an innovative strategy for transforming education. Federations are groups of schools that share staffing, resources, professional development, curriculum development, leadership and management. The Department for Children, Schools and Families (DCSF), previously part of the Department for Education and Skills (DfES), defined federations in two ways:

- The definition as invoked in the 2002 Education Act, which allows for the creation of a single governing body or a joint governing body committee across two or more schools.
- A group of schools with a formal (i.e. written) agreement to work together to raise standards, promote inclusion, find new ways of approaching teaching and learning and build capacity between schools in a coherent manner. This will be brought about in part through structural changes in leadership and management, in many instances by making use of the joint governance arrangements invoked in the 2002 Act.

The former have been termed 'hard' federations, as they are tightly coupled and sit at the more formal end of the spectrum of school-to-school collaboration arrangements. Across all types of federations, it is generally recognized that there is a need for high levels of trust, co-operation and confidence for the partnerships to work effectively (Lindsay et al, 2007).

While networks or federations are not new, the extent of current networking activity between schools is growing. Contemporary evidence would suggest that investment in school-to-school partnerships offers some educational return (Lindsay et al, 2007). Where schools are in networks there is increasing evidence that they are able to raise their collective performance and improve outcomes. The evidence also shows that they are also more able to innovate and to share practice for the benefit of all schools (Jackson and Temperley, 2007).

It is suggested that the power of networking is maximized within a diverse set of schools rather than a homogeneous group:

> Network theory tells us that homogeneous networks, characterised by close proximity (e.g. the same local authority) limit the extent of different ideas to which the members are exposed and consequently restrict their thoughts and actions to a small repertoire of options. In contrast, networks developed among educators from diverse educational backgrounds, of diverse professional belief systems, and with diverse professional practices or teaching assignments provide a rich source of new ideas and new possibilities and a foundation for experiments in practice. This sort of experimentation holds the potential for profound improvement.
>
> (Smylie and Hart, 1999:6)

There is ample evidence from both the public and private sector that networks and partnerships are a powerful means of achieving knowledge creation (Sullivan and Skelcher, 2003). Also evidence shows that such networks and partnerships provide particularly powerful mechanisms of self-renewal during periods of extensive change (OECD, 2000). The OECD research (2000) shows that creating collaborative structures around schools is more likely to result in deeper organisational learning both collectively and individually.

The two examples that follow explore distributed leadership *between* schools, in the case of a federation, and *outside* schools, in the case of an extended school.

Ninestiles School

Context

Ninestiles is an 11–18 foundation, inner city, Technology College with 1,500 pupils in Birmingham. The school has been a key partner in a three-school federation and most recently a two-school federation. Since 1988 the school has successfully increased its 5 A*–C grade GCSE results from 6 per cent in 1988 to 75 per cent in 2006. It has driven the change process through a number of strategies focusing on the core elements of effective teaching and learning, assessment for learning and curriculum entitlement and choice. This is combined with a service approach to pupils and a focus on distributed leadership practice.

The school was one of the first in the country to enter into a formal federation with two other schools in the Birmingham area. Ninestiles linked with George Dixon International School in Edgbaston, and with Waverley School in Birmingham in 2003. The International School was formed in September 2002 when two secondary schools, which shared the same site, amalgamated.

The International School serves a community that experiences levels of socio-economic deprivation which are amongst the highest nationally. The proportion of pupils entitled to free school meals is substantially above average. The pupil population is predominantly white; with a low proportion of ethnic mix. The proportion of the pupils with special educational needs is in line with national averages. The results at the International School were ranked fourth worse in the country. At its lowest level only 9 per cent of students achieved A–C grades at GCSE. In 2006 the school achieved

36 per cent GCSE A–C grades with a value-added score of 1,046 against an LA average of 1,002. In 2007 it was one of the most improved schools in the country.

Waverley School is a smaller than average secondary school. It gained Humanities Specialist status in September 2006. The school serves an area of high deprivation. There is a cultural and ethnic mix of students. The majority of students are either from Bangladeshi or Pakistani origin. Over 80 per cent of students use English as an additional language. Eighty-five per cent of pupils are from a Muslim background. Over half are eligible for free school meals. The proportion of students with learning difficulties at the school is over 50 per cent.

In February 2001 Waverley was put into special measures and was about to close. It had falling rolls and a fairly bleak future. During 2001 it became part of the federation with the International School and Ninestiles. Students achieving five A–C grades rose to 15 per cent in 2003 and to 27 per cent in 2006.

Distributed leadership

The federation was established in 2003 with the prime aim of improving performance and raising standards at Waverley and the International School. With the support of Federation resources and, in particular its leadership expertise, both schools embarked on substantial internal reorganisation. The subsequent transformation in performance has been attributed to the establishment of strong leadership and management at each school, along with a new and permanent core of new teachers.

The head teacher at Ninestiles and key members of his senior leadership team, and a wide range of other staff, spent time at both schools building up confidence, sharing expertise and creating new leadership capacity. The model of distributed leadership between the schools was one that relied heavily on coaching, mentoring and advising. The approach was one of sharing leadership expertise across the three schools rather than superimposing a particular approach or type of leadership practice.

Through a process of dialogue, demonstration and discussion, new leadership structures, roles and approaches were established at the International School and the Waverley School. Leadership support from Ninestiles was offered at the point of need, and it was always recognised that this support would be time-limited. Leadership practice and expertise was actively shared between the three schools with the prime aim of putting in place structures and processes that would improve learning and teaching. The head and his staff spent time at each school working with teachers, students, governors and the senior leadership team to put in place the foundation for improvement.

Commentary

The federation came to an end in 2005 and both the International School and Waverley School continue to perform well. The new leadership structures and processes are now well established and there is strong leadership at each of the schools. The recent OfSTED inspection at Waverley noted that 'standards have improved considerably at key stage 4. The proportion of students who achieve A–C grades at GCSE is well above the national average (OfSTED, 2007:5). It also stated that leadership and management were good, and that staff are enthusiastic and committed to the school.

At the International School there has been a significant rise in pupils achieving five A–C grades at GCSE, rising from 34 per cent in 2004 to 50 per cent in 2006. Attendance across the school also increased from 84.1 per cent in 2004 to 88.1 per cent in 2006. The OfSTED report noted that 'leadership and management are very good. The leadership provided by the head-teacher is excellent backed up by the very good leadership of other key staff' (OfSTED, 2005: 5).

Since 2005, Ninestiles has been in a federation with Central Technology School in Gloucester. In 2003 the school had secured 21 per cent A–C at GCSE and in 2006 GCSE results improved dramatically. Ninestiles is providing leadership support, expertise and guidance, which has contributed significantly to the school to re-establishing itself and to improved performance.

The latest OfSTED report notes:

> the remarkable improvements seen at Central Technology College are a testament to good leadership and management. The executive head-teacher and head teacher, along with the senior leadership team and governors set the tone. They have the highest expectations and recognize that outstanding behaviour and outstanding teaching form the cornerstone of effective learning.
> (OfSTED, 2007:8)

The report also notes:

> the improvement since the last inspection has been outstanding. This remarkable improvement has come about as a result of outstanding leadership of the executive head teacher and the new head teacher. This leadership has put in place a substantial improvement programme that has led to a dramatic turnaround in the school's performance. Central to this improvement has been the collaborative work with advanced skills teachers and middle leaders from Ninestiles.
>
> (OfSTED, 2007:5)

An evaluation of the 'Federations Programme' (Lindsay et al, 2007) found that the two key factors of success across federations were distributed leadership and a relentless focus on teaching and learning. The evaluation highlighted the key features of effective leadership as being: a focus on instructional improvement; building collaboration and good relationships; having clear aims and objectives; developing collegiality, trust and effective communications, and extending leadership responsibility.

Beauchamp College

Context

In 2005 the DfES published their 'Extended Schools Prospectus' detailing the Department's vision that, by 2010, all children should have access to well-organised, safe and stimulating activities before and after school in order to provide children and young people with a wider range of experiences and to make a real difference to their chances at school. The prospectus set out a core offer of services that all children should be able to access through schools by 2010.

The core offer includes:

- a varied menu of study support activities such as homework, sports and music clubs;
- high-quality childcare provided on primary school sites or through local providers, with supervised transfer arrangements where appropriate, available 8am–6pm all year round;
- parenting support, including information sessions for parents at key transition points, parenting programmes run with the

support of other children's services, and family learning sessions
to allow children to learn with their parents;

- identifying children with particular needs to ensure swift and
  easy referral to a wide range of specialist support services such as
  speech and language therapy, child and adolescent mental health
  services, family support services, intensive behaviour support
  and sexual health services;
- ICT, sports and arts facilities, and adult learning for the wider
  community.

This prospectus made it clear that schools needed to work closely
with parents and children's services in order to provide a fully
operational extended schools service. To date over 3,800 schools (one
in six) are providing access to extended services in partnership with
voluntary, private and independent providers.

Beauchamp College is a 14–19 co-educational high performing
specialist school in Leicestershire with over 2,000 students. It was
formerly a grammar school dating back 600 years. The school serves
a large ethnic population and almost 67 per cent of the students are
from ethnic minority families, so the College community is rich and
diverse. It has been given the responsibility of working in partnership with other secondary and primary schools in the local and wider
community. Its role is to share and disseminate good practice, and
provide relevant and challenging research or training opportunities
for staff and students in order to further improve the quality of
teaching and learning.

In 2006, 77 per cent of students passed five or more subjects at
GCSE at grade C or above. These results place the school in the top
255 nationally of schools in similar circumstances. The sixth form
has nearly 1,100 students and examination results are consistently
high. The College was inspected in November 2003, and received a
very positive report encapsulated in 82 per cent of lessons judged to
be good or better and 47 per cent rated excellent.

Distributed leadership

As a Community College there are over 2,500 part-time students
taking part in over 500 day and evening classes – recreational, cultural and academic. Staff total over 300 and they include administrative, clerical, technical, cleaning and catering staff. Consequently,
the model of leadership at the College is widely distributed and relies

heavily upon clear communication mechanisms to keep staff updated and informed.

The leadership team comprises the principal, three assistant principals (one of whom is the business manager) and two senior team leaders with responsibility for research and training. Targeted students are assigned a mentor. All secretarial staff mentor year 11 students. There is a key stage 5 office team that looks after the sixth form students academic and pastoral needs. The associate staff span the various responsibilities associated with providing extended services which include full day care for children, a playgroup, before- or after-school clubs, adult learning, community access to college facilities, and youth clubs. The College's Childcare Centre offers integrated childcare and education for children under five years of age, family support and support for parents to access opportunities for work and training. The College has about fifty affiliated societies and many day-time activities.

The decision-making and leadership at the College are widely distributed and rely heavily upon partnerships and local forums. There is a Local Residents' Forum and a Stakeholders' Forum. In addition the college makes sure it is represented on other forums such as business, early years, etc. The model of distributed leadership operating outside the school with the local community is shown in Fig. 8.1.

Extended schools cannot afford to be insular therefore the College has to connect with many organisations and agencies outside the school. With such a complex organisation staff need thinking and planning time as well as support from colleagues. For this reason the Extended Service Vice Principal has set up a 'dream team', which recruits extended service managers nationally to identify and share good practice. The College is currently working with Leicester University and Leicester Grammar School to be one of the competition and training sites for the 2012 Olympic Games.

Commentary

The model of distributed leadership in operation at the College is one that encompasses a large and diverse range of staff both within and outside the college. The Principal underlines the importance of 'distributed followership' in order for distributed leadership to work effectively. While there are high degrees of autonomy and responsibility these are coupled with clear lines of accountability. The model

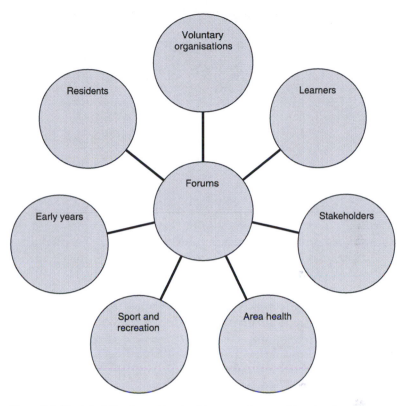

Figure 8.1 Model of distributed leadership operating outside school.

works because all staff are committed to the idea of extended service provision and understand the role they play plus the individual contribution that they make.

The extended school service agenda is so complex and diverse that it has provided the opportunity for the College to be innovative and to take risks. The College offers a full IT consultancy service and has a sports hall and leisure faculties that are open to the public. It currently trains teachers and offers NVQ qualifications.

Students are encouraged to believe it is 'cool to learn' and the distributed leadership model also extends to students. The College involves students in decision-making and core leadership activities. There is an emphasis upon student voice at the College. Students are involved in research, learning walks and lesson observations. There are two student governors and the student committee meets on a weekly basis. The ideas and decisions are then communicated to the leadership team.

As Richard Parker, the Principal of Beauchamp College notes:

> . . . a visionary, inspiring and motivating culture of distributed leadership, the opportunity to pursue ideas, even if they may collapse in glorious failure, which rarely happens, is vigorously promoted. To be listening and consultative allows the leadership team, and in fact all staff, to take risks and innovate knowing they have 100% support.

Overview

Each of the cases highlights, in very different ways, how schools are purposefully and deliberately altering leadership practices with the central aim of improving student learning outcomes. The cases illustrate how restructuring has allowed more individuals to be able to influence change and to be part of innovation. In many of the examples, there is evidence to suggest that distributing leadership more widely, more creatively and more purposefully had resulted in positive organisational outcomes. While direct links between leadership practice and student learning outcomes are notoriously difficult to measure or prove, these case studies do point towards a positive relationship between distributed leadership and learning.

As Spillane and Diamond (2007:163) point out 'research on leadership and management from a distributed perspective is still very much pre-adolescent. Much work remains to be done.' They suggest that one way forward might be to 'design research tools and processes that can be used by school leaders alongside those who work on leadership and management development'.

The cases presented here are not empirical research findings but illustrations of current leadership practice in schools. They offer insights into the ways in which schools view distributed leadership and the difference they feel that broad-based leadership has made to their performance. As the following quotations from head teachers illustrate, there is a perception that distributed leadership has resulted in improvements in teaching and learning which have in turn been converted into positive student learning outcomes.

> Over the last three years we've changed from being a traditional school where the teachers did everything and there were teachers and support staff, now it's come together a lot more, there's not a

thick black line between teachers and support staff because we've got support staff mentoring, we've got support staff as link tutors. This has ensured that individual learning and progress is clearly targeted. This has made a difference to achievement.

It's the distributed leadership model, completely, you talk to the majority of teaching staff in school they've all got responsibility for something, there's very much not a massive gap between senior leadership and teaching staff. Closing this gap has meant a consistent, coordinated focus on raising achievement, which has worked.

Leadership is spread across the schools – everybody has a very clear role. In terms of the impact of this on the quality of teaching – well, it's gone up, OfSTED shows and our results show it!

The findings from this small group of schools suggest that fattening leadership structures and moving leadership practice closer to classroom practice can benefit learning. It is not simply that the roles are reallocated that seems to make a difference but *how* the roles or responsibilities are rearranged that seems to matter most. It is not simply a case of randomly reshuffling the original leadership pack. The purposeful design and orchestration of leadership responsibilities, so that there is closer proximity to learning and teaching, is of paramount importance. It is the particular pattern or configuration of leadership distribution that influences the 'quality of leadership practice' (Leithwood et al, 2007).

Spillane and Diamond (2007:154) highlight the centrality of leadership practice in their work. They show that 'practice is not reduced to a set of behaviours or actions that can be extracted from place and time', but that practice is embedded in time and in context. Therefore it is only by appreciating the backdrop of restructuring and redesign that distributed leadership practice can ever be fully understood. This is because changes in structure alter the balance of relationships, and inevitably change the nature of interactions. Distributed leadership practice is fundamentally located in the interactions of individuals and groups.

The cases in this book illustrate how restructuring or reorganising leadership responsibilities in some schools has resulted in new organisational routines, expectations and behaviours. These new routines, expectations and behaviours have influenced a change in culture that, in turn, has impacted upon organisational performance and outcomes.

The cases highlight eight characteristics of distributed leadership.

Box 8.1   Eight Characteristics of Distributed Leadership

Vision is a unifying force:

- A clearly articulated vision which is equally shared among all members exerts a cohesive force. It is what allows progress to be made without diverging or going off course.

Leaders have expert rather than formal authority:

- Leadership shifts according to need; leadership generally resides with the person who has expert authority for the task or activity.

Collaborative teams formed for specific purposes:

- The teams have fluid membership, which changes according to the task, the roles, and the requisite talent. These are non-permanent teams.

Communities of practice emerge:

- Although collaborative activities tend to disband, the communities of practice maintain their affiliation long after the task, and often connect with each other in order to brainstorm about future needs and potential collaborative configurations.

Individuals perceive themselves as stakeholders:

- All individual team members are willing and able to assume leadership positions, when needed.

The organisational goals are disaggregated:

- The tasks needed to achieve the mission can be broken down into component parts and distributed to the teams best able to achieve the tasks.

Distributed roles and tasks:

- They take place in different time zones, places, and under widely divergent conditions.

Enquiry is central to change and development:

- Enquiry is central to organisational renewal and innovation. The ultimate goal of distributed leadership is knowledge creation and organisational improvement.

These eight characteristics highlight the potential of distributed leadership as a catalyst of organisational change and development. In all organisations there will be formal and informal structures that can either support each other or actively work against each other. The next section considers the way in which formal and informal structure can support or suppress distributed leadership.

Formal and informal structures

In order to maximise a school's creative potential and learning capability, it is crucial to understand the interplay between the formal, designed structures and the informal, self-generating networks or groupings. The formal structures comprise the rules, boundaries and regulations superimposed upon relationships within an organisation. They are reflected in documents and artefacts, such as the organisational chart, the budget, planning documents and a wide variety of policies.

In schools, the developmental plan, the self-evaluation framework document, the staffing structure and the timetable are strong structural frames that shape and determine acceptable ways of interacting and working. These structural arrangements determine behaviour within an organisation; they signal what is expected and what is rewarded. As we have seen in earlier chapters, if structures are changed, it can radically redefine both individual and collective professional practices.

In contrast, informal structures are 'fluid and fluctuating networks of communication' (Capra, 2004:110). They are the non-verbal forms of engagement and interaction through which tacit knowledge is generated and shared. Within these informal networks are certain shared boundaries of meaning that only those belonging to the informal structure can access and fully understand. Within schools, informal networks are often related to age, gender or even common social, religious or sporting activities. They are informal groupings that bring individuals together in ways that are not determined by the dominant structure and are voluntary. Informal networks depend on a common practice, shared values or experience. In all organisations there is a continual *interplay* between the formal and informal structures. In some organisations this interplay will be positive, particularly where the energy created by the informal networks feeds into the formal structure. In other organisations the informal networks will be seen as undermining and distracting attention from the core or central organisational purpose.

Within every organisation there is a cluster of interconnected individuals that comprise a community of practice. If channelled properly, informal structures or networks can contribute greatly to knowledge creation and, as the next chapter will demonstrate, can create the conditions for informal interaction within and between schools.

If an organisation is a social system capable of learning, the question must be *how do we maximise an organisation's capability and capacity to learn?* If informal structures are communities of practice, *how do we create the conditions where communities of practice flourish and grow?* If distributed leadership equates with new forms of informal interconnection, *how do we create the opportunities for distributed leadership to emerge?*

The next chapter focuses on the relationship between distributed leadership and knowledge creation. It focuses on the way in which specific forms of distributed leadership practice can amplify the knowledge created both within and across schools.

Chapter 9

Distributed leadership and knowledge creation

> In a knowledge-based economy, the new coin of the realm is learning.
>
> (Robert Reich)

Introduction

As societies face the challenges brought about by globalisation and the new technologies, the critical importance of innovation and knowledge creation has become clear to all. Most leaders would say that their main challenge is one of generating and sustaining innovation in order to keep the competitive edge. This is particularly true in education, where the economic and social costs if the system fails to innovate will be substantial.

As Fullan et al (2007) note, 'education needs a system that will support the day to day transformation of instruction for all students – a system that is both practical and powerful': a system that will provide high quality learning experiences for all students in all settings. But how do we generate this system? If knowledge creation is the key to transformation, will major shifts and changes in schools and school systems be needed? Krogh et al (2006:7) suggest that effective knowledge creation depends on an *enabling context*, a shared space that fosters emerging relationships. They suggest that knowledge creation is best supported and nurtured by forming communities based on social processes where individuals collaborate and work together. These 'micro-communities of knowledge' provide the shared space that encourages and nurtures participation on many different levels.

It is clear that neither bureaucracies nor hierarchies provide the optimum structures for knowledge creation. Instead organisations that are interdependent and collaborative are more likely to be the enabling contexts required for knowledge creation to occur. These *collaborative enterprises* will be networked, virtual ecosystems consisting of actual and potential allies and partners (Heckscher, 2007:25). They will have extended, dynamic and diverse systems of interaction requiring leadership practices that go far beyond the current structural boundaries of teams, partnerships or networks.

The collaborative enterprise will sustain two sets of relationships – the *vertical* and the *horizontal*. The dominant organisational infrastructure will depend on strong collaborative teams, both real and virtual. The distinguishing mark of the collaborative enterprise will be its *interdependence*, its *networking* and its *adaptability*, rather than its conformity or its mark of authority. It will be an organisation where the quality of leadership practice will matter more than leadership roles or positions.

Leadership will be required in the collaborative enterprise that is flexible, responsive and able to realign itself to a changing environment and changing needs. Distributed leadership has these features and it is argued will play a major role in organisations of the future as the hierarchical structures and hierarchical forms of leadership fall away (Harris, 2006). In their place will emerge forms of leadership practice based on relationships, rather than roles or job descriptions.

Relationships are at the heart of knowledge creation as they provide the means of sharing and understanding. Nonaka and Takeuchi (1995:84) argue that the organisation moves from tacit knowledge to explicit knowledge by 'sharing, creating concepts, justifying concepts, building an archetype, and cross-leveling knowledge'. So the knowledge spiral continues. In organisations where this occurs, knowledge is *co-constructed* through interactions and between people. As a result learning takes place.

The fragility of knowledge creation means that it needs to be supported by a *leadership circuitry* or infrastructure that enables it to happen. This infrastructure should allow the sharing of tacit knowledge and effective conversations across various organisational levels. It is suggested that distributed leadership provides an infrastructure for professional interaction, co-construction and learning to occur at multiple levels.

Distributed leadership and knowledge creation

In their work on distributed leadership practice, Spillane and Diamond (2007) illustrate the power of co-construction through conversations and interactions between teachers. Their work focuses on the relationship between leadership and classroom practice and the way leadership is distributed *across leader, follower and the context*. Their work makes the relationship between instruction and leadership explicit and shows how one aspect of instruction, the school subject, is a potentially powerful explanatory variable in leadership practice.

From a distributed perspective, Spillane and Diamond (2007:32) argue that:

> . . . aspects of the situation such as organizational routines and tools are not simply a backdrop or an accessory for school leadership and management practice. Rather by framing interactions among leaders and followers, organizational routines and tools are *a core defining element of practice*.

Their position is that leadership practice takes shape in these interactions and that the routines and tools can transform leadership practice over time.

However, it is also clear that organisational structures can influence the situation, routines and tools that are thought to be most appropriate and ultimately valued. The structural configuration of leadership roles and responsibilities will ultimately determine and shape the nature and type of leadership interactions within the organisation. A hierarchical model of leadership provides a very different organisational architecture for professional interaction than a school with both a vertical and a lateral or horizontal leadership structure.

The basic point here is to agree with Spillane and Diamond (2007) that leadership is a function of the 'interactions between leaders, followers and their situation', but to argue that these interactions are heavily influenced and framed by organisational structures and settings. In other words that the *practice* of leadership cannot be seen in isolation from the organisational structure that ultimately determines, and to some extent dictates, the types of routines, practices and norms in each context or setting that are seen as meaningful.

Spillane and Diamond (2007:164) claim that the important question is not *that* leadership is distributed but *how* it is distributed. Taking a normative rather than an analytical stance on distributed leadership means exploring *how* leadership is distributed. It implies looking at the ways in which different organisational forms detract or add to patterns of leadership distribution. It also means attending to organisational design and focusing on whether knowledge is *created* or *re-cycled*.

Currently distributed leadership is theoretically rich and empirically poor. As argued in previous chapters, we undoubtedly need more specific, deep empirical studies of distributed leadership (Harris, 2007b). However the empirical evidence we have, to date, and the evidence that is emerging is encouraging, if not definitive. It points towards a positive relationship between distributed leadership and organisational learning (Harris, 2007a; Leithwood et al, 2007).

The evidence is also beginning to show that the patterns of distribution make a difference to student learning outcomes. Research by Day et al (2007:17) found that 'substantial leadership distribution was very important to a school's success in improving pupil outcomes'. The findings showed that distributed leadership, where it went beyond routine delegation, cultivated a sense of ownership and agency on the part of staff. The project found that leadership distribution commonly took one of two broad forms or patterns. The first pattern, *consultative distribution*, featured considerable participation of key staff in providing information and advice on school-wide decisions, but final decisions were retained by those in formal leadership positions. The second pattern, *decisional distribution*, awarded full responsibility and a high degree of autonomy to teacher leaders for all decisions in a designated area of responsibility.

The project also found that the leadership structures in the most effective schools were becoming 'fatter' rather than flatter and the relationship between vertical and horizontal leadership was porous and interchangeable. The research evidence showed that the principals or heads largely determined the nature and pattern of leadership distribution in their schools. The patterns they chose were determined by three main influences:

a   their *personal* view of leadership (e.g. need for control);
b   their own stage of *development* as a leader;
c   their estimates of the *readiness of their staff* to take on greater leadership responsibilities (Day et al, 2007:19).

Spillane and Diamond (2007:164) suggest 'that a distributed take on leadership is not an effective prescription for effective leadership in and of itself'. But if we have sufficient evidence that certain organisational forms are more effective than others, why should we shy away from some prediction or prescription? As Leithwood et al (2006a, 2006b) and Day et al (2007) have shown, it is possible to identify such patterns.

The remainder of this chapter focuses on *how* distributed leadership contributes to *knowledge creation and organisational growth*. It looks at *how* schools are deliberately distributing leadership functions in order to build leadership capacity. The chapter draws upon findings from an empirical study of distributed or deep leadership practices.

Distributed leadership in practice[1]

In 2005, the Specialist Schools and Academies Trust, in England, established a network of schools committed to the creation of new professional practices and system-wide transformation. The 'Development and Research' (D and R)[2] networks are viewed as integral to system wide renewal and transformation within England, and they are all actively engaged in innovation, dissemination and co-construction. There are currently 55 hub schools, which are the catalysts and the focal point for the school-to-school networks, and over 376 D and R schools across the country.

The establishment of D and R networks is consistent with the idea of knowledge creation developed by Nonaka and Takeuchi (1995). The D and R networks are premised on the notion that new ideas, research breakthroughs and applications arise anywhere in the sector,

1 This section draws upon a chapter entitled 'Distributed Leadership and Knowledge Creation' in a forthcoming book by Leithwood et al (2008): *Distributed Leadership*, Netherlands, Springer Press. I am grateful to the 'Specialist Schools and Academies Trust' for allowing me to draw upon their D and R work; however the views expressed in this paper do not represent the views held by the Specialist Schools and Academies Trust. In particular, I wish to acknowledge the contribution of Professor David Hargreaves and also thank Sue Williamson, Emma Sims and Kai Valcher at the Specialist Schools and Academies Trust and Gill Ireson and Toby Greany at the National College for School Leadership in England for allowing me to draw upon their research work.
2 The D and R networks are funded by the Specialist Schools and Academies Trust: http://www.specialistschools.org.uk/.

not just within the boundaries of formal R and D activities. In R and D networks, users play more of a role in the process of knowledge creation and dissemination.

In school-to-school D and R networks, practitioners lead and disseminate new ideas, they are central to the 'sparking, shaping, validating and spreading of innovation' (Bentley and Gillinson, 2007:4). As Chesbrough (2003) argues, 'it's about harnessing the most effective sources of innovation – from wherever they are derived. This is not just about ideas but rather about their realisation.' In his model of 'open innovation', users are involved in shaping the service and are active participants in knowledge creation.

The 'D and R' model is premised on the idea of open innovation as the aim of the practitioner networks is to create new knowledge. The networks are guided by the '3 Ds Model' – they are decentralised (in their structure), disciplined (in the way that innovation is organised) and distributed (in the construction of the innovation agenda) (Hargreaves, 2003).

While there is no overall blueprint for the networks, schools have been required to lay out clear plans for innovation that had the core purpose of creating new and better practices in learning. The latest group of D and R networks have focused their activities on distributed or deep leadership. Hargreaves (2006:2) suggests that 'deep leadership means re-designing education so that, through a culture of personalization and co-construction with shared leadership, the school secures deep experience, deep support and deep learning for all its students'.

During 2007 an empirical study was undertaken to provide summative and formative feedback about the impact of the 'deep leadership' work in schools (Harris, 2008). In particular the research focused upon the nature, type and forms of leadership required to promote and sustain knowledge creation. It explored how school leaders were creating and sustaining a culture of co-construction and provided evidence of various forms and configurations of distributed leadership practice.

The research utilised data from the D and R network database and also collected in-depth case study data[3] from 11 D and R schools. These schools were selected for the project on the basis that they were engaged in innovative leadership practice and were committed to

3 A full account of methodology can be found in Harris et al (2008).

working with other schools in a decentralized, disciplined and distributed manner. All the schools demonstrated a commitment to sharing practice and supporting other schools that are aspiring to gain expertise in the area of distributed or deep leadership.

A range of data was collected that included semi-structured interviews with key leaders involved in the work (i.e. head, hub co-ordinator and other staff members, students) in each school to explore the way in which deep leadership is being implemented and sustained. The data provided insights into the way in which schools were conceptualising leadership practice and actively reorganising structures so that alternative forms of leadership practice could emerge. It was clear that the hub schools were catalysts for action and played an important role in ensuring that schools continued to push the boundaries of their leadership re-design process.

A model of distributed leadership practice

The data from the study showed that through their various activities schools were involved in vertical or lateral leadership differentiation. They were actively seeking to 'stretch leadership' (Spillane, 2006), by creating the opportunities and the 'spaces' for greater participation in leadership within and across schools. In his work Weick (1976) talks about loose and tightly coupled systems. In his seminal paper, Weick (1976) argues that the coupling imagery provides organisational researchers with a powerful new way of talking about organisational complexity. Loose coupling conveys an image that separate parts are *somehow attached* and that *each retains some identity and* separateness.

This imagery is particularly helpful in representing different forms of distributed leadership practice. Unlike the model of distributed leadership practice provided by Spillane and Diamond (2007), which focuses upon the relationship between leaders, followers and their situation, the model outlined below focuses on the structural alignment, composition and patterns of distributed leadership practice. It is primarily concerned with outlining various ways in which schools are rearranging leadership practice.

The two axes of the model represent firstly, tight *versus* loose organisational coupling and secondly, diffuse (uncoordinated) *versus* deep (co-ordinated) forms of leadership distribution. This typology provides four different forms of distributed leadership practice:

	Loose Organisational Coupling		
Diffuse DL	**Ad Hoc Distribution** *Flexible structure but* *uncoordinated practice*	**Autonomous Distribution** *Flexible structure and deep* *coordinated practice*	**Deep DL**
	Autocratic Distribution *Rigid structure and random* *practice*	**Additive Distribution** *Rigid structure with limited but* *coordinated forms of practice*	
	Tight Organisational Coupling		

Figure 9.1 Models of distribution.

- *Ad Hoc* – a more flexible, lateral and loose organisational structure has been created but the distributed leadership practice is uncoordinated and random. As a consequence the benefits to the organisation are limited.
- *Autocratic* – structures remain relatively unchanged but participation and involvement in development work is encouraged. However, it is restricted by the existing structure therefore its impact is limited.
- *Additive* – structures remain relatively unchanged, but opportunities have been deliberately created for limited forms of developmental and innovative work. This work is coordinated but its impact on the organisation is additive rather than transformative.
- *Ambitious* – a more flexible, lateral and loose organisational structure has been created with the prime purpose of generating innovation and change. The leadership work is coordinated and disseminated in ways that impact positively upon the organisation and other organisations. There is clear commitment to co-construction and to transformational processes.

The D and R schools are clear examples of organisations that were loosely but purposefully coupled. As Weick (1976:7) points out, 'such organisational configuration can be good for swift and substantial localised adaptation – any one element can adjust to and modify a local unique contingency without affecting the whole system'.

The data showed that all of the D and R schools had abandoned certain practices, they had actively restructured to maximise teacher-to-teacher interaction, and a number were trying to develop more sophisticated forms of student leadership. The teacher-to-teacher element was an important dimension of their work as well as the drive to increase collaboration and staff cohesiveness. The next section provides some illustrations of the type of work the D and R schools had undertaken to distribute leadership more widely and to embed it more deeply.

Distributed leadership practice[4]

The following vignettes illustrate some of the ways in which D and R schools are restructuring and redefining leadership practice. Many are part-way through this process.

Box 9.1   Distributed leadership, school A

School A

Context

School A is an 11–19 comprehensive with over 1,200 pupils. It is located in a suburban area where the socio-economic profile is mixed. The school performs very well. It is a diverse school with more than 82 per cent of pupils coming from ethnic minority backgrounds. There are over 40 languages spoken in the school. It has just moved into a new building (£30 million) with a campus-like structure based on faculty buildings, which has provided the opportunity to redesign the leadership structures.

---

4 I am grateful to the schools and the NCSL and SSAT for allowing me to draw upon their 'Deep Leadership' work.

Distributed leadership

The school has deliberately flattened and extended its leadership team. It has moved from one head teacher and two deputies to one head teacher, three deputy heads, and eight assistant heads (including one job-share). Each assistant head leads a faculty or phase with one non-teacher as a key support. The school has also tried to distribute leadership through subject teams and has tried to inculcate a culture where leadership goes right down to the classroom teacher.

The school also has a junior leadership team where students apply for the post and shadow the senior leadership team members. This opportunity is open to all students through a formal application process. The two leadership teams take responsibility for joint planning and decision-making. There is succession planning and training for both leadership teams that is provided at the school and in a residential setting. The school invests heavily in leadership development and training of both staff and students.

Impact

The junior leadership team has had a major impact on the extent to which students feel that they are part of decision-making in the school. They feel that through this form of distributed leadership that they have a 'voice' and can influence the direction of the school. The school staff are also more involved in decision-making and feel that they can take an active role in leading innovation and change.

Box 9.2 Distributed leadership, school B

School B

Context

School B is a large secondary school in a rural area with 1,950 pupils. The socio-economic indicators suggest that the school is in an area with some deprivation. There is an even spread of ability among pupils with about 10 per cent of pupils having

English as a second language and 10 per cent being eligible for free school meals. Standards of pupil achievement are steadily improving.

Distributed leadership

Leadership has been distributed among the 'four deeps' identified by Hargreaves (2006):

- Deep Leadership – principal, vice principal and business manager;
- Deep Experience – assistant principal, consultant, tech leaders (emphasis on new technologies);
- Deep Learning – assistant principal; consultant;
- Deep Support – three assistant principals; those with Key Stage responsibilities; head of sixth form.

There is a core Leadership Team consisting of principal, vice principal and business manager, with assistant principals There is also an extended team that consists of the core plus a range of consultants. Consultants take a leading role in CPD including sophisticated approaches to observing teaching, outreach work to other schools and conferences.

New teachers are introduced to the processes and principles of distributed leadership during their induction. The school has been particularly successful in attracting high quality staff because of its reputation for distributed leadership practice.

Impact   *Org. outcomes*

There has been a shift within the school towards a professional learning culture. Personalised learning has led to learning-to-learn formats for teachers to use, techniques for accelerated learning and the adoption of assessment for learning. The structural re-alignment around the four 'deeps' has had a positive impact on learning and pupil achievement. In addition, assessment-for-learning is now embedded in the school and this would not have been possible without the structural changes that have located leadership practices closer to teaching and learning.

Box 9.3   Distributed leadership, school C

School C

Context

School C is just short of 1,600 on roll. It is a comprehensive school serving the full range of ability in what might seem a 'leafy suburb', but this is not reflected in the intake of the school. It is a high-performing school and seen as 'a very good school poised to become outstanding' by OfSTED.

Distributed leadership

Leadership has been dramatically reconfigured within the school. The leadership team has been restructured to reflect the discourse of deep leadership. Distributed leadership is a core part of its philosophy and at the core of trying to change things. The school wanted to develop the leadership capacity and potential of all staff and therefore set up their own year-long Emerging Leaders course for support staff using the leadership framework they had developed. The aim was to maximise the leadership potential of those in support roles and to generate leadership capacity through internal, targeted training.

Impact   Org. outcomes

There are closer working relationships between support staff and teaching staff as both groups see themselves as potential leaders. Also accountability has deepened as a result of distributed leadership. In particular, as a result of the leadership training, subject leaders have taken greater responsibility for working with other teachers to create new materials, ideas and knowledge. Both teachers and support staff tend to see themselves as accountable for educational attainment in the school. This demonstrates a new mindset and a more collaborative approach to raising attainment.

Box 9.4   Distributed leadership, school D

School D

School D is a primary school in a suburban setting. It is a school that has grown significantly in terms of student numbers in the last five years. During that time the leadership structure and practices within the school have changed.

Distributed leadership

The leadership responsibilities have been extended from just the head teacher to a model of a head and several co-deputies. Each deputy takes on the role for one half-term. They all have more than five years' experience, and when they are not in the deputy head role they are full-time classroom teachers. As the Head is a regional leader of a Leadership Network and is out of school two days per week, a co-head has been appointed from within the staff. This means that the leadership team is structurally flexible and relies on extended membership that is constantly renewing itself, as members come into the team and leave the team.

In addition the school is now leading a network of 30 schools that are interested in system redesign and distributed forms of leadership practice between schools. The aim is to create a network of schools that are actively innovating around leadership practice and trying different models and configurations of leadership activity.

Impact

The flexible and extended leadership team has encouraged teachers to engage more with decision-making processes and to take on temporary leadership roles. The links to schools within the network have created the opportunity for trialling alternative innovative practices between schools and to look for ways of connecting leaders at different levels across the network.

The school has become much more outward facing and is generally recognized as a source of innovative practice. Teachers tend to stay in the school and are able to combine leadership experience without relinquishing teaching duties permanently. This has created a vibrant interface between leadership and learning that has had a positive impact on teachers and students at the school.

Bentley and Gillinson (2007:4) argue that the potential of 'organizing traditional R and D into D and R has the potential to have powerful effects on performance'. There is emerging evidence that the D and R networks are beginning to have a positive impact at three levels (Harris, 2007a):

- Firstly, at the level of the *individual*, where there is enhanced professional practice.
- Secondly, at the level of the *school* where there is much greater commitment, willingness and energy for sharing and implementing new ideas.
- Thirdly, *teaching and learning practices* are being influenced by the D and R networks, particularly the processes and practices associated with personalised learning.

There is evidence that the new leadership arrangements prompted by the D and R networks are providing a platform for knowledge creation, application and dissemination. The new leadership structures are encouraging teachers to share knowledge with other teachers, both within their own school and across the network. In this respect, D and R networks provide a powerful platform for the leverage of knowledge and the acceleration of innovation.

Nonaka and Takeuchi (1995) identify two sets of dynamics that drive the process of knowledge amplification:

- Converting tacit into explicit knowledge
- Moving knowledge from the individual level to the group, organisational and inter-organisational levels.

The latter requires some form of knowledge leveraging which is very visible within the practices of the D and R networks. This *leveragable body of knowledge* is all the knowledge available to the community via all participants in the system. The repository for 'captured' knowledge, the knowledge base, must provide feedback in support of its own continued development and evolution. It must also support the following types of interactions from each of the participants within the system.

Effective knowledge creation depends on an enabling context or a *knowledge space* where knowledge is shared and where the tacit becomes the explicit. D and R networks seem to be powerful 'knowledge spaces' (Krogh et al, 2006). They are encouraging collaboration, communication and dialogue in a supportive context. They are essentially 'micro-communities of knowledge' (Krogh et al, 2006). They are fluid, rather than fixed, continually evolving with accumulated collective experience.

Wenger (1998) proposes that when learning in communities of practice, participants gradually absorb and are absorbed in a *culture of practice* giving them exemplars, leading to shared meanings, a sense of belonging and increased understanding. D and R networks are distinguished by their emphasis on group or collective learning, their mutual trust and professional respect.

Hargreaves (2003:9) suggests that 'a network increases the pool of ideas on which any member can draw', and that 'networks extend and enlarge the communities of practice with enormous potential benefits'. There is emerging evidence that the D and R networks provide the spaces for knowledge creation, and that this impacts positively upon instructional processes.

Wenger (1998) suggests that effective change processes consciously facilitate negotiation of meaning. In this model, negotiation consists of two interrelated components:

- *Reification* – This process is central to every practice. It involves taking that which is abstract and turning it into a 'congealed' form, represented for example in documents and symbols. Reification is essential for preventing fluid and informal group activity from getting in the way of co-ordination and mutual understanding. Reification on its own, and insufficiently supported, is not able to support the learning process, however.

  > But the power of reification – its succinctness, its portability, its potential physical presence, its focusing effect – is also its danger . . . Procedures can hide broader meanings in blind sequences of operations. And the knowledge of a

formula can lead to the illusion that one fully understands the processes it describes.

(Wenger, 1998:61)

• *Participation* – the second element in the negotiation of meaning requires active involvement in social processes. It involves participants not just in translating the reified description/prescription into embodied experience, but in recontextualising its meaning. Wenger describes participation as essential for getting around the potential stiffness (or, alternatively, the ambiguity) of reification.

> . . . If we believe that people in organisations contribute to organisational goals by participating inventively in practices that can never be fully captured by institutionalised processes. . . . we will have to value the work of community building and make sure that participants have access to the resources necessary to learn what they need to learn in order to take actions and make decisions that fully engage their own knowledgeability.
>
> (Wenger, 1998:10)

Crucially, Wenger describes the relationship between reification and participation as a dialectical one: neither element can be considered in isolation if the learning or change process is to be helpfully understood.

> Explicit knowledge is . . . not freed from the tacit. Formal processes are not freed from the informal. In fact, in terms of meaningfulness, the opposite is more likely . . . In general, viewed as reification, a more abstract formulation will require more intense and specific participation to remain meaningful, not less.
>
> (Wenger, 1998:67)

Wenger calls the successful interaction of reification and participation the *alignment of individuals* with the communal learning task. Alignment requires the ability to co-ordinate perspectives and actions in order to direct energies to a common purpose. The challenge of alignment, Wenger suggests, is to connect local efforts to broader styles and discourses in ways that allow learners to invest their energy in them.

The most effective D and R networks align individuals with a common, shared and clear set of objectives. They are also able to generate and create new knowledge that has a direct impact on the quality of learning in schools. As their central focus is personalised learning, the instructional benefits are always at the heart of any collaborative or networked activity. Co-construction ultimately defines and shapes the way they collaborate, share and generate new knowledge.

Distributed leadership and knowledge creation

Effective knowledge creation depends on an enabling context or environment (Krogh et al, 2006). Such an organisational context can be physical, virtual, mental or hyper-virtual. Knowledge creation requires the necessary context or 'knowledge space' where knowledge is shared and where the tacit becomes the explicit. D and R networks are powerful 'knowledge spaces'. They enable collaboration, communication and dialogue to occur in a supportive context that contributes to knowledge creation.

This knowledge creation is based upon social processes and working as groups or 'micro-communities of knowledge' (Krogh et al, 2006). Micro-communities are characterised initially by shared interests, but over time they assume sets of behaviours and practices that allow them to become a coherent group that can solve problems and generate ideas.

D and R networks are micro-communities of knowledge; they are fluid, rather than fixed, continually evolving with accumulated collective experience. Learning within D and R networks involves active deconstruction of knowledge through reflection and analysis, and its reconstruction in a particular context or with a particular focus in mind.

There is emerging evidence that the D and R networks provide the spaces for knowledge creation, which impacts positively upon instructional processes. However we need to know much more about the nature, processes and impact of D and R networks. We need to know whether D and R networks can be scaled up, if they are sustainable in the mid to long term, whether and how the networks connect to each other and the effect such 'macro-communities' of practice might have on system.

Work is already underway to address some of these questions and to illuminate the way in which D and R networks are contributing to change and innovation at the school and system level. D and R networks are creating the spaces for teachers to work with teachers to co-construct knowledge and to generate new insights into instruction. They are providing opportunities for teachers to interact, to reach beyond their own experience and knowledge by working collaboratively.

Choo (1998) suggests that organisational innovations 'germinate from the seeds of tacit knowledge', and that implicit knowledge generates new value when it is made explicit. As knowledge moves from an individual to an organisation in the form of teams, groups and networks it can provide the shared context where knowledge creation takes place. It provides a social context in which the meaning of objects, problems, events and artefacts are constructed and negotiated.

This view accords with knowledge-based constructivism where social networks, trustful relationships and collaboration promote the co-construction of knowledge and practices. It also reflects the central concepts associated with socially situated cognition, social learning (Resnick and Spillane, 2006) and communities of practice. Lave and Wenger (1991) suggest that all learning is contextual, embedded in a social and physical environment. They assert that situated learning 'is not an educational form, much less a pedagogical strategy' (1991, p 40).

Effective knowledge creation depends on an enabling context or environment (Krogh et al, 2006). Such an organisational context can be physical, virtual, mental or hyper-virtual. Knowledge creation requires the necessary context or 'knowledge space' where knowledge is shared and where the tacit becomes the explicit. This knowledge creation is based upon social processes and working as groups or 'micro-communities of knowledge' (Krogh et al, 2006). Micro-communities are characterised initially by shared interests, but over time they assume sets of behaviours and practices that allow them to become a coherent group which can problem solve and build organisational capacity.

Capacity building

Without a clear focus on 'capacity', a school will be unable to sustain continuous improvement efforts, or to manage change effectively. From a relatively simple perspective, capacity building is concerned with providing opportunities for people to work together in a new way. Collegial relations are therefore at the core of capacity building. One of the distinguishing features of schools that are failing is the sheer absence of any professional community, discourse and trust. Within improving schools, a climate of collaboration exists and there is a collective commitment to work together. This climate is not simply given but is the deliberate result of discussion, development and dialogue amongst those working within the organisation.

Capacity building is about ensuring that the school is a 'self-developing force' (Senge et al, 1999) through investing in those school and classroom-level conditions that promote development and change (Hopkins, Harris and Jackson, 1997). The limitations of 'top-down' and 'bottom-up' change are well documented. Both fail to recognise that unless the internal conditions within a school are predisposed to change and development, irrespective of how 'good' the new initiative or change is, it will inevitably flounder.

But what does capacity building look and feel like in practice? The driving force here, although not stated explicitly, is the expansion or thickening of leadership. Hopkins and Jackson (2003) point us towards some useful central concepts and perspectives that offer an operational definition of capacity. The first is the central importance of the *people*, the leaders, educational professionals and students, and the expansion of their contributions. A second relates to the alignment and synergies created when internal arrangements, connections and *teams* are working optimally. A third corresponds to the organisational arrangements (the 'programme coherence' and the 'internal networks'), which support *personal* and *interpersonal* capacity development.

The fourth is more subtle, but crucially important. It is the territory of shared values, social cohesion, *trust*, well-being, moral purpose, involvement, care, valuing and being valued – which is the operational field of 'leadership'. The two key components of a capacity-building model are the professional learning community (the people, interpersonal and organisational arrangements working in developmental or learning synergy) and leadership capacity as the route to generating the social cohesion and trust to make this happen.

In this sense, capacity building is concerned with developing the conditions, skills and abilities to manage and facilitate productive school-level change. It also necessitates a particular form of leadership to generate school improvement, change and development. This leadership is one that focuses upon learning, both organisational and individual, and one that invests in a community of learning – parents, teachers, pupils and governors.

Harris and Lambert (2003:4) argue that leadership capacity building can be defined as 'broad-based, skilful involvement in the work of leadership'. This perspective involves two critical dimensions of involvement – breadth and skilfulness:

1   *Broad-based involvement* – involving many people in the work of leadership. This involves teachers, parents, pupils, community members, LEA personnel, universities.
2   *Skilful involvement* – a comprehensive understanding and demonstrated proficiency by participants of leadership dispositions, knowledge and skills.

This constructivist approach to leadership creates the opportunities to surface and mediate perceptions; to inquire about and generate ideas together; to seek to reflect upon and make sense of work in the light of shared beliefs and new information; and to create actions that grow out of these new understandings.

The evidence from the school-improvement literature indicates that schools that are improving tend to be marked by a constant interchange of professional dialogue at both formal and informal levels. Also they have ways of working that encourage teachers to work together towards shared goals. There is a body of evidence that demonstrates that teachers work most effectively when they are supported by other teachers and work together collegially. Hopkins and Jackson (2003) note that 'successful schools create collaborative environments which encourages involvement, professional development, mutual support and assistance in problem solving'.

Recent assessments of the relationship between leadership and school improvement imply that giving others responsibility and developing others is the best possible way of the school moving forward (Day, Harris and Hadfield, 1999). One of the most congruent findings from recent studies of effective leadership is that the authority to lead need not be located in the person of the leader but can be distributed both within the school and across schools.

As we have seen earlier, evidence would suggest that where this distributed form of leadership is in place there is greater potential for building the internal capacity for change. This form of leadership necessarily requires relinquishing the idea of structure as control and instead viewing structure as the vehicle for empowering others. For this approach to work requires a high degree of trust, as trust is essential to support the leadership climate. As Evans (1998:183) notes:

> Trust is the essential link between leader and led, vital to people's job, status functions and loyalty, vital to fellowship. It is doubly important when organisations are reaching rapid improvement, which requires exceptional effort and competence, and doubly so again in organisations like schools that offer few motivators.

It is suggested therefore that the type of leadership which leads to school improvement is located between and among individuals within an organisation: it belongs to a broad group of people, including non-teaching staff, parents and students who all contribute to the school's distinctive culture and community.

The following diagram summarises the dimensions of capacity building in schools. It places student achievement and engagement in learning at the centre, as this has to be the core purpose of any efforts to build capacity or improve schools. There is a clear focus on the use of evidence to inform learning and teaching processes, and an emphasis upon collaboration and distributed leadership as the organisational infrastructure that can best support learning and teaching.

The model underlines the reciprocal nature of the relationships between the various capacity building dimensions. The prime aim is to generate the capacity that will sustain a professional learning community.

Capacity-Building Schools

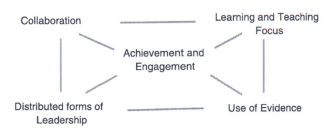

Figure 9.2 Capacity-building schools.

Professional learning communities

Throughout this chapter the term 'distributed leadership' has deliberately focused upon the quality of relationships and the connections among individuals within and between schools. Distributed leadership is leadership separated from person, role and status. It is chiefly concerned with creating a leadership infrastructure that is dynamic rather than static and that will result in improved learning outcomes. As Stoll and Seashore Louis (2007) point out, the ultimate goal is to link professional learning communities to improvements in teaching and learning.

The literature on professional learning communities repeatedly gives attention to shared forms of leadership. Sergiovanni (1992:214) explains that 'the sources of authority for leadership are embedded in shared ideas', not in the power of position.

Mutual respect and understanding are the fundamental requirements for this kind of workplace culture. Teachers find help, support, and trust as a result of developing warm relationships with each other. If one goal of reform is to provide appropriate learning environments for students, then teachers, too, need an environment that values and supports hard work, the acceptance of challenging tasks, risk taking, and the promotion of growth. Sharing their personal practice contributes to creating such a setting.

In summary, the necessary features of a professional learning community are as follows (adapted from Morrisey, 2000):

- the collegial and facilitative participation of the head or principal, who *shares* leadership – and thus, power and authority – through inviting staff input in decision making;
- a *shared* vision that is developed from staff's unswerving commitment to students' learning, and that is consistently articulated and referenced for the staff's work;
- *collective* learning among staff and application of that learning to solutions that address students' needs;
- *review* of each teacher's classroom behaviour by peers as a feedback and assistance activity to support individual and community improvement; and
- physical conditions and human *capacities* that support such an operation.

The evidence points to the importance of teachers working together and learning together in generating the capacity for change. However, while teacher collaboration may be highly desirable it is not always easy to achieve in practice. In many ways the design and organisation of schools present the biggest challenge to teacher collaboration and the building of learning communities. Teachers who do want to work together often find the barriers of time, competing tasks and physical geography difficult to overcome.

In summary, schools that improve and continue to improve, invest in the life of the school as a *learning organisation*, where members are constantly striving to seek new ways of improving their practice (Senge, 1990). An optimal learning environment provides teachers with opportunities to work and learn together. It promotes sharing ideas and the open exchange of opinions and experiences.

Teacher collaboration, reflection, enquiry and partnership are ways of building capacity for school improvement. Constructing and participating in the building of professional communities in schools is by its nature a vibrant form of professional development. Lave and Wenger (1991) propose that when learning in communities of practice, participants gradually absorb and are absorbed in a 'culture of practice', giving them exemplars, leading to shared meanings, a sense of belonging and increased understanding.

Organisational theorists have long emphasised the differentiated and even fragmented nature of organisations (Martin and Frost, 1996). Many writers have explored the issue of organisational complexity and differentiation in some depth (Lima, 2007). According to Jablin (1987) organisational complexity develops through two processes of internal differentiation: 'vertical differentiation' (the number of different hierarchical processes in an organisation relative to its size), and 'horizontal differentiation' (the number of department divisions within it).

Vertical and horizontal differentiation

It is clear that many schools, districts and systems are now actively engaged in both vertical and horizontal differentiation. They are deliberately restructuring leadership functions, redefining leadership roles and rearranging leadership responsibilities. They are seeking to provide the *spaces* and opportunities for knowledge creation to take place.

While it is clear that extending and enhancing leadership should not be regarded as the only or even main strategy for transforming schools and school systems, it remains a powerful lever. Evidence shows that high-performing and complex organisations are highly differentiated, and have leadership structures that provide maximum flexibility for organisational growth and change. They are organisations that have optimised vertical and horizontal leadership differentiation.

If we are really serious about system transformation, we need to do things differently. The process of school and system transformation is unlikely to be achieved without some radical, long-term change in leadership structures and practices. The danger is that token, superficial changes will be implemented instead of the deep-rooted changes.

If this happens, then new 'old leadership practices' will simply be recreated and this will actively undermine any transformational process. As Fullan et al (2007) note: 'What is needed now is proactive leadership in which individuals and groups seek ways of connecting to adjacent layers of the system. In the end distributed leadership will make it work.' As we have seen in previous chapters, many schools have already recognised this need, and are already moving towards alternative forms of leadership structures and practices.

The question is whether they are *moving fast enough?*. The pace of technological change is quickening, as are the demands on schools and school systems. Our present ways of organising are fast becoming outmoded, yet we seem hypnotised with current structures and ways of leading. It is possible that the new or alternative leadership approaches may not be any better than those currently in operation. We won't know this unless we change the structures and the practice.

The next chapter focuses on the possibilities and potential for future leadership. It returns to the idea of the organisation as a *living system, interconnected, dynamic and complex*. It argues that the organisations of the future will be networked and nested within larger systems. It suggests that future leadership will need to be distributed both within and across networks and systems.

Chapter 10

Future leadership

The difficulty lies, not in the new ideas, but in escaping from the old ones.

(John Maynard Keynes, 1936)

There is nothing more difficult than to take the lead in the introduction of a new order of things.

(Niccolò Machiavelli, *The Prince*)

Introduction

In the course of history, society has occasionally to make a sharp break with old habits and move to new ways of functioning. For example, the dramatic changes in thinking about physics at the turn of the twentieth century constituted a revolutionary break with previous understanding and knowledge. The exploration of the atomic and subatomic world resulted in major shift, a 'paradigm shift', that according to Kuhn (1962) occurs in *discontinuous, revolutionary* breaks in understanding.

In the world of contemporary physics, it is suggested that a new paradigm is emerging. This new paradigm is 'a holistic worldview, seeing the world as an integrated whole rather than a dissociated collection of parts' (Capra, 1996:6). It has also been referred to as an *'ecological view'*, in the sense that this viewpoint recognises the fundamental independence of all phenomena. As Capra notes (1996:6), 'ecological awareness recognises the fact that as individuals and societies we are all embedded in and ultimately dependent on the cyclical processes of nature'. It recognises the intrinsic value of all living beings and the prominence of integration over self-assertion.

Amid dramatic changes in technology and global commerce, those working in business organisations have begun to recognise the need for integration over self-assertion. In Western industrial culture, in particular, it could be argued that there has been an over-emphasis on self-assertion and competition. The social structures best suited to excessive self-assertion are hierarchically ordered, as this is the optimum way of exerting power and control. (Berkun, 2007)

As outlined in Chapter 1, global capital and its handmaiden, technology, have given rise to a new economy that has transformed traditional relationships of power. Dominant social functions are increasingly organised around networks, and in this 'network society' as Castells (1996) calls it, the new power is influence through integration and interdependence, rather than power over others.

The basic argument here is that the new organisational forms, whether hospitals, businesses or schools, will be structured upon various forms of collaboration and supported by different networking activities. As Capra (2002:106) reinforces,

. . . most large corporations today exist as decentralised networks of smaller units . . . they are connected to networks of small and medium-term businesses that serve subcontractors and suppliers. The various parts of those corporate networks continually recombine and interlink, cooperating and competing with one another at the same time.

The cases in the book illustrate clearly how schools are actively dismantling the hierarchical model of leadership. Although the nature of the restructuring varies from school to school, there is a consistent move towards creating smaller, interlinked sub-units, whether they are colleges, consultation groups or teams. The prime purpose of this reorganisation is to allow greater involvement in leadership activities, and to provide a platform for innovation and knowledge creation. In short, the purpose of redesign is to secure improved organisational performance.

The system's view of organisational learning emphasises that the most effective way to enhance an organisation's performance is to allow people to look beyond the immediate context, and to appreciate the impact of their actions upon others (and vice versa). According to Peter Senge (1990:3), learning organisations are:

... organizations where people continually expand their capacity to create the results they truly desire, where new and expansive patterns of thinking are nurtured, where collective aspiration is set free, and where people are continually learning to see the whole together.

The basic rationale for such organisations is that in situations of rapid change, only those that are flexible, adaptive and productive will excel. For this to happen, it is argued, organisations need to 'discover how to tap people's commitment and capacity to learn at all levels' Senge (1990:3). While all people have the capacity to learn, the structures in which they have to function are often not conducive to reflection and engagement. Furthermore, people may lack the tools and guiding ideas to make sense of the situations they face.

Senge (1990:340) argues that learning organisations require *a new view of leadership*. He sees the traditional view of leaders as deriving from a deeply individualistic and non-systemic worldview. At its centre the traditional view of leadership 'is based on assumptions of people's powerlessness, their lack of personal vision and inability to master the forces of change, deficits which can be remedied only by a few great leaders'. Against this traditional view, he sets an alternative view of leadership that is preoccupied with *subtler and more important tasks*.

In a learning organisation, leaders are designers, stewards and teachers. They are responsible for building organisations, and are people who continually expand their capabilities to understand complexity, clarify vision, and improve shared mental models. Many of the qualities associated with the learning organisation are reflected in a model of distributed leadership. In learning organisations, leadership is identified by the quality of people's interactions rather than their position. Improved performance relies on what people do, rather than who people are within the organisation.

So why is it that in many organisations, the traditional model of leadership prevails? Why is it that many organisations remain locked into leadership structures and practices that are least likely to secure sustainable improvement? Part of the answer lies in an adherence to the existing power structure, a deep-rooted personal vested interest in keeping the structures as they are, a misplaced emotional attachment to the status quo.

Why would you want to relinquish your leadership position, remuneration or status? Why would you take a risk that the new organisational form would be any better, any more effective, than the current form? Why leap into the unknown when the current position is so much safer, so much more predictable?

Jumping the Curve

One explanation for the deep resistance to major organisational change can be found in *Jumping the Curve* by Imparato and Harari (1994). Their work claims that while the wave of social and economic change that started in the middle of the century is accelerating and spreading, there is anxiety and a sense of disarray within many organisations about *exactly* how to respond.

They point out that organisations are often self-trapping because of an adherence or even loyalty to past ways of working. As Imparato and Harari (1994) note, 'memories of past success have too often handicapped substantial progress'. Yet it is clear that piecemeal solutions in the face of current change forces simply will not work: 'nothing short of radical transformation will suffice' (Imparato and Harari, 1994:14).

Jumping the Curve offers a model of organisational success that is not locked into normative or habitual ways of thinking about change and innovation. It challenges the normal idea of business development that describes the natural life cycle of an organisation as a sigmoid curve. This assumes that a company will start at the bottom of the S curve and will slowly make its way upwards, going through different loops before eventually reaching the very top.

This model assumes that organisations that are successful travel along the same curve. In other words they have routine ways of doing things that make them successful and they continue to do more of what they do well. Yet recent evidence would suggest that successful companies actually discard patterns of working when the moment requires it. Leaders of such companies recognise the moment in time when old ways of working have to be jettisoned and new ways of working embraced. This is what Imparato and Harari (2007) call 'jumping the curve'.

'Jumping the curve' requires organisations to shift their priorities from stabilising to innovating. This involves recognising that innovation and creativity, rather than control or order, are the key levers of market survival and profitability. Imparato and Harari (2007) suggest that the first organising principle is to 'look a customer ahead'. The second organising principle is to build the organisation around the 'accumulated intelligence' of the employees. This requires changing priorities from building mass and size to growing organisational competence. They argue, as does this book, that such knowledge creation is the key to transformation.

Organisations of the future that succeed will have developed both the structures and the cultures to ensure that those they serve are satisfied and valued. The third and fourth principles of jumping the curve are therefore concerned with 'ensuring that those who live the values and ideals of the organisation are the most valued', and 'treating the customer as the final arbiter of service and product quality by offering an unconditional guarantee of complete satisfaction' (Imparato and Harari, 2007:76).

The costs of not 'jumping the curve' are fairly plain to see. If we look, for example, at the fortunes of Marks & Spencer, it is clear that this is a company that lost its market share primarily because it persisted with old patterns and a traditional business formula in a changing environment. As Bevan (2007:5) summarises,

> Marks & Spencer, 114 years old and the second most profitable retailer in the world, the subject of three Harvard Business School case studies, five times winner of the Queen's Award for Export Achievement and with cupboards groaning with trophies for managerial excellence, steamed on full throttle towards the iceberg.

While the competition had reinvented itself during the recession of the early 1990s, Marks & Spencer scarcely noticed. Its amalgam of problems included complacency, no real sense of the competition, a lack of innovation (particularly in new technologies) and an inward looking leadership style that thrived on upholding, at all costs, the traditional values of the company. The company paid little attention to leadership succession planning at the time of its demise and were convinced, even when presented with evidence to the contrary, that the company was doing well.

As the new chief executive of Marks & Spencer noted, 'if you don't look outside the window every day then the world will pass you by', and it was his contention that the revival of the company would not be achieved by simply returning to the safety of the past: something more was required. Whether Marks & Spencer has completely 'jumped the curve' is as yet uncertain, although all the signs are very favourable and suggest that this is not another false dawn for the company. Their market position is stronger, but the legacy of losing their way will continue to dominate their psyche for some time to come, whatever successes they achieve.

In contrast, Motorola are an example of a company that has been pretty adept at jumping the curve. Founded in 1928 as a manufacturer of car radios, it moved with every successful shift in technology. It moved from car radios to walkie-talkies, to TVs, to integrated circuits, to microchips and wireless communication. They remain one of the biggest and most profitable companies in the mobile communication industry today.

So what are the implications here, if any, for schools? It is dangerous to draw too many comparisons with the business world, where profit remains the main motivation. The examples from the business world, however, do offer two possible scenarios for schools of the future. One scenario is to adhere to *current practices* despite the changing environment, and then have to make frenzied changes to save the organisation. The second scenario is to make calculated but *bold changes* when the time is right, thus protecting the organisation and safeguarding its future.

The implications are clear. The time for tinkering, adjusting or amending existing leadership practice in schools is running out. The old structures are buckling under the weight of the external environment and the demand for higher performance. Raising the bar and closing the gap will require schools, like other organisations, to 'jump the curve' if they are to remain relevant, effective and integral to society.

This will require a departure from previous practice – a break with the past. So what are we currently doing to redesign our schools so they are ready to jump the curve? A huge capital programme is planned across schools in England in the next ten years. How far is this programme a major opportunity to rethink what schools should be, and how they might function in the twenty-first century?

Building Schools for the Future

Building Schools for the Future (BSF) represents a new approach to capital investment. It is bringing together significant investment in buildings and in ICT (Information and Communications Technology) over the coming years to support the government's educational reform agenda. The Government is committed to devolve significant funds – about £3 billion in 2005/2006 – to local authorities (LAs) and schools to spend on maintaining and improving their school buildings. But it also wants to promote a step-change in the quality of provision. That is the focus of BSF.

BSF is worth £2.2 billion in its first year (2005/2006). It aims to ensure that secondary pupils learn in twenty-first-century facilities. Investment will be rolled out to every part of England over 15 waves, subject to future public spending decisions:

- By 2011, every LA in England will have received funding to renew at least the school in greatest need – many will have major rebuilding and remodelling projects (at least three schools) underway through BSF, and the remainder will have received resources through the Academies programme or Targeted Capital Fund.
- By 2016, major rebuilding and remodelling projects (at least three schools) will have started in every LA.

The question is how radical are the new designs? How far do the new buildings reflect the learning needs of young people in the future? To what extent will the new organisational structures provide the flexibility required to accommodate technological advances that have not been thought of as yet? To what extent are we building schools for failure rather than the future?

The danger is that we will build new 'old' schools that may be architecturally more interesting, brighter, technologically more up to date, but essentially schools as we would recognise them: essentially, as they largely look today and have done since the turn of the century. It is clear that organisational structures both enhance and restrict organisational functioning. They can either promote or limit innovation and creativity.

In Chapter 9 it was argued that schools of the future would need to move from hierarchical to networked organisations. In Chapter 7 it was suggested that the old-style, bureaucratic form of leadership was being replaced with lateral and distributed leadership forms. The school as a network organisation has a centre or core which, as Beare (2006: 38) suggests, has 'tight control over technical quality, research, and development, major investment decisions planning, training and coordination activities'. In the school of the future the 'essential product is leadership' (Toffler, 1985:129), and this leadership will be widely distributed to make the organisation flexible and responsive to change.

'Schools of the Future' will not need permanent, factory-like quarters but we are in danger of building them. As Beare (2006:39) warns:

> . . . premises like that can be inhibiting, if not dysfunctional . . . it may be counter-productive to require a student to spend most of her learning time within a fenced paddock, for learning can take place anywhere, and frequently off campus or in a place not normally described as a school. Computer access, portable computers (laptops and notebooks) hand-held devices and portable digital storage space make it possible to function through an interconnected web of learning sites and through a network of resource people.

In summary, it is not possible to offer a definitive answer to how schools 'jump the curve', but it is clear that building new 'old' buildings are not the answer. It is also clear that leadership geared towards the needs of the new 'old' schools is unlikely to result in educational transformation. If, as Wheatley (1999) argues, our present ways of organising are outmoded and that many organisations aren't working so well, what does this imply for future schooling and future leadership?

Future schooling

The OECD (2005) document, *Schooling for Tomorrow*, presents six scenarios of future schooling. These scenarios are descriptive pictures or stories aimed at helping individuals or organisations understand the complexities and uncertainties of their wider context. The scenarios are intended to help organisations prepare themselves for the future, so that potential threats can be avoided and opportunities may be undertaken. The first two scenarios focus on maintaining the status quo. The next two focus on re-schooling whilst the final two focus on de-schooling.

In summary the six scenarios outlined by the OECD (2005:6–11) are as follows:

- *Bureaucratic school systems continue* is built on the premise that there will be a continuation of powerfully bureaucratic systems, where there are strong pressures towards uniformity and resistance to radical change. In this scenario schools are highly distinct institutions, knitted together with complex administrative arrangements. Priority would be given to administration and the capacity to handle accountability pressures, with a strong emphasis upon efficiency.

- *Teacher exodus – the meltdown scenario* is premised on the fact that there would be a major crisis of teacher shortages triggered by a rapidly ageing profession exacerbated by low teacher morale, plus buoyant opportunities in more attractive graduate jobs. In this scenario, crisis management predominates and a fortress mentality prevails.

- *Schools as core social centres* – here, the school enjoys widespread recognition as the most effective bulwark against social, family and community fragmentation. The school is now defined by collective and community tasks, which results in shared responsibility between schools and community bodies. Management and leadership are complex, as the school is a dynamic interplay with diverse community interests. Leadership is widely distributed and collective.

- *Schools as focused learning organisations* implies that schools are revitalised around a strong knowledge agenda rather than a social agenda, in a culture of high quality experimentation, diversity and innovation. ICT is used extensively alongside other learning media, traditional and new. Knowledge management is central, and the very great majority of schools view themselves as 'learning organisations'. The schools have flat structures, using teams, networks and diverse sources of expertise. Decision-making is rooted within schools and the profession, with the close involvement of other stakeholders and agencies.

- *Learning networks and the network society* suggests the abandonment of schools in favour of a multitude of learning networks, quickened by the extensive possibilities of powerful, inexpensive ICT. The deinstitutionalisation and even dismantling of school systems is part of the emerging 'network society'. With schooling assured through interlocking networks, authority becomes widely distributed and diffused. There is no longer a reliance on particular professionals called 'teachers', as demarcation of roles breaks down. Greater expression is given to learning for different cultures and values through networks of community interest.

- *Extending the market model* means that existing market features in education become significantly extended as governments encourage diversification in a broader environment of market-led change. This is fuelled by the dissatisfaction of 'strategic consumers' in cultures where schooling is commonly viewed as a private as well as a public good. Many new providers enter the learning market encouraged by reforms of funding structures, incentives and regulation. Entrepreneurial management modes are more prominent and there is reduced role for public education authorities. New learning professionals – public, private, full-time, part-time – are created in the learning markets, and the most valued learning is determined by choices and demands.

There is evidence to suggest that many schools are already operating as core social centres. The demands of 'Every Child Matters' and 'Extended Schools' have necessitated more multi-agency involvement and more partnership work across different organisations. There is also evidence that schools are operating as focused learning organisations and being creative about learning practices. It is clear that many schools are already operating in sophisticated networks. These may not exactly equate with the fifth scenario as yet, but it is without question the future reality of schooling.

Schools are already functioning as networks, operating as federations, and collaborative partnerships. An example of the force of networking and school-led system change is captured in the 'Leading Edge' schools in England. The Leading Edge Partnership programme was aligned with the Specialist Schools programme in 2005. The programme is one of the options open to High Performing Specialist Schools, and is now the only route into the programme. The Leading Edge Partnership programme is about secondary schools working together to address some of the most critical learning challenges facing the education system. These partnerships focus on:

- raising the performance of schools that are struggling to raise standards;
- closing the achievement gap by addressing issues of underperformance among groups of pupils from poorer socio-economic backgrounds and from particular ethnic minority groups.

There are currently 215 Leading Edge Partnerships across nearly 100 local authorities (LAs). Their work is securing system-level change through collaborative, collective and distributed leadership. Recent research (Harris et al, 2007a) has emphasised that the degree of distribution is a major factor in a school's success as a social centre.

The least effective schools tended to have inflexible leadership structures aimed at control rather than innovation. In contrast, the effective schools were characterised by the extended use of support staff and extended leadership teams.

Where schools were most effective they had created *new leadership structures* that manifested themselves in new roles, new responsibilities, new teams and new ways of working. Where little attention had been paid to creating new leadership structures, channels and processes, there was little evidence of improvement. In short, the leadership practices were not 'fit for purpose', and the schools were locked into a leadership structure that was too inflexible to accommodate the new demands and requirements of the changing external environment.

From mechanistic to organic

Most organisational commentators would suggest that the twenty-first century organisation is organic rather than mechanistic. It is essentially a living system, where mutual support guarantees survival. Wheatley (1999:7) suggests that 'we have just begun the process of discovering and inventing the new organisational forms that will inhabit the twenty-first century'. This may be true but we have some very clear indicators of the underlying principles of a twenty-first century organisation.

The organisations of the future will require that systems are understood as *whole* systems, organisations will be networks and attention will be given to relationships within those networks. As Wheatley (1999:11) points out, 'in the quantum world, *relationship* is the key determinant of everything'. As highlighted earlier in the chapter, organisational theory is now being influenced by science, which shows that the survival and growth of systems are sustained by complex networks combined with high levels of autonomy for individuals within the system. From large ecosystems down to the smallest microbial colony, interdependence, autonomy and flexibility to change are the key principles of system design.

Beare (2006: 64) offers a number of features of the future 'school', which align with the idea of the organisation as a 'living system'. These features have been adapted as follows:

1   *The borderless school* – the self-contained, stand-alone school located in splendid isolation is superseded by a process-orientated,

learning brokerage enterprise with permeable boundaries, providing programmes to each of its students through a network of places, agencies and people.

2   *The technological environment* – the book and paper-bound school has been comprehensively computerised, its administrative processes are all IT-run, every student and learning space is equipped with access to a computer, and all its academic profiling and learning outcomes data is consistently stored and accessible to anyone in the network.

3   *The networked curriculum* – the old steps and stages, linear, age-related, subject-orientated curriculum has been replaced by a thinking curriculum based on developing competences, thinking skills and new information.

4   *Student groupings* – age cohort classes have given way to the grouping of students according to their learning needs, their location and orientation to learning. The learning provision is available 24/7.

5   *Workforce diversity* – the workforce supporting teaching and learning is diverse, and includes multi-agency provision and support. Configurations of support are guided by the learner, and a portfolio of online and face-to-face tutoring keeps the individual learner on track.

6   *Networked leadership structures* – the old organisational structures have disappeared – the schooling enterprise is now a network organisation that travels light, has fuzzy boundaries, is organised for interactivity and transacts its work through strategic alliances and partnerships (Beare, 2006:66).

The future schools will be organisations whose functions are carried out in satellite or subsidiary units, each with its own team and operating mode. Some organisations will diversify radically with extended community services. Others will specialise and draw together resources and agencies best suited to specialist needs. As Beare (2006) points out, some schools will run subsidiary campuses and offer adult learning programmes or vocational training. Variation rather than uniformity will be the watchword of the future school.

Co-ordination will be achieved through leadership teams who connect and safeguard the core purpose of the organisation, i.e. maximising learning. These teams will be loosely coupled in terms of location and tightly coupled in terms of core purpose and professional standards. In future schools, leadership will be widely distributed.

Future leadership

In the fluid, boundary-less organisation of the future, what will leadership look like, how will it function, where will it be located? Part of the adherence to old structures and models of leadership is a belief that letting go might result in chaos or a loss of order that might not be regained. Yet, in the natural world, disorder is a new source of order.

Prigogine (1985) uses the term 'dissipative structures' to describe new forms that are derived from the ebbing away or loss of other forms. As an award-winning chemist, Prigogine (1985) discovered that dissipative activity or loss was necessary to create a new order. Dissipation did not result in the death of a system, it was part of the process by which a system let go of its present form so that it could regroup and reorganise in a form better suited to the demands of the changed environment.

If we are to develop new forms of organisational behaviour then leadership is more important than ever. The configuration or patterns of influence will determine the nature of the organisation and the organisational outcomes. As Wheatley (1999:131) suggests:

> When chaos has banged down the door and is tossing us around the room it is difficult to believe that clear principles are sufficient. In this chaotic world we need leaders. But we don't need bosses. We need leaders to help us support the clear identity that lights the dark moments of confusion.

If leaders are to influence change in these new organisational forms, it is critical that they remember that they are working within a web of relationships and that, to change the system, it 'needs to learn more about itself from itself' (Wheatley, 1999:131). Leadership in the future will be more connected to its environment and clients, more connected to its people everywhere in the system, and more aware that its primary purpose is to facilitate change.

Within the new sciences, in living systems theory, quantum physics, chaos and complexity theory, we are able to observe life's dependence on participation. The participatory nature of reality means that we need to focus greater attention on relationships, interactions and interdependencies. As Wheatley (1999:164) notes, 'nothing exists independent of its relationships, whether looking at subatomic particles or human affairs'.

Future leadership will be concerned primarily with *participation and relationships* rather than leadership skills, competencies or abilities. Future leaders will be spread across the organisation, and will constantly nurture and fuel new knowledge, new ways of knowing and new ways of doing. Future leadership requires a radical shift in thinking about organisational design and the forms of leadership required within new organisational forms.

Future leadership will need to be broad-based, dynamic, shared, diffuse and responsive. Leadership practice will be located within complex sets of interactions and influences. It is here that we rejoin Spillane's (2006) particular conception of distributed leadership as leadership that is *stretched* or shared.

It is suggested that future leadership will have the following features or dimensions:

- **Collective rather than individualistic**

Leadership of the future will be premised on multiple rather than individual leadership. As organisations become more complex, diffuse and networked, forms of direction and influence will be required to respond to quickly shifting and changing environments. Multiple sources or points of leadership will be needed within the organisation to ensure it is both sensitive and responsive to change.

- **Inclusive, flexible and self-renewing**

Future leadership will no longer be divided into fixed roles and responsibilities. Patterns of leadership responsibility will ebb and flow. Leadership functions and actions will depend on organisational need, and the patterns of leadership activity will be flexible enough to regroup and remobilise around particular issues or areas for development. Future leadership will be self-renewing, as new sources of leadership expertise and capability will be actively sought within the organisation.

- **Responsive to internal demands**

The leadership of the future will be driven as much by internal demands as by the external environment. It will be highly sensitive to changes within the organisation. With broader and deeper forms of leadership activity there will be more opportunity to pick up early signals within the organisation of any potential destabilisation. With more emphasis upon the relational aspects of leadership, any potential issues can be highlighted early, and any opportunities quickly taken.

- **Driven by learning before results**

The educational organisations of the future will be networked, diffuse and partly virtual. For each learner there will be a different configuration of learning support, an individualised and personalised learning programme. Therefore the leadership of the future will be primarily concerned with maximising synergies and connectivity across different parts of the learning network. The focus will be on the quality, nature and extent of learning provision as well as the organisation's ability to create its own knowledge.

- **Multi-layered and networked**

The leadership patterns of the future will be determined by the configuration of the network of provision. The complex nature of organisations in the future will mean that it will be multi-layered and inevitably networked locally, nationally and globally. The co-ordination of leadership activity will most likely be undertaken laterally rather than vertically, and leadership functions and responsibilities will fluctuate with the needs of the organisation. Leadership patterns will be non-permanent within the organisation.

- **Leadership capabilities rather than roles**

There will be a prime focus on leadership capability and capacity building within and between new organisational forms. Attention will be paid to maximising leadership capacity by securing broad-based leadership with high degrees of involvement, autonomy and decision-making responsibilities.

- **Seeks out new leadership spaces**

A prime purpose of future leaders will be to seek out opportunities to generate new leadership capacity. They will seek the organisational spaces where new knowledge can be formulated and where new practices can be developed. They will seek ways of turning tacit knowledge into explicit knowledge, and will concentrate on knowledge transfer within the organisation.

- **'Best fit' rather than 'will fit'**

Future leadership will be arranged into patterns that fit the needs of the organisation at any one time. The focus will be on 'best fit' rather than 'will fit'. Hence any leadership practices that no longer suit the organisation will be abandoned, and new leadership configurations assembled or co-constructed to meet the new needs of the organisation.

- **Puts innovation at the centre**

Future leadership will ultimately be 'one customer ahead'. It will be primarily and chiefly concerned with knowledge creation, and with producing innovation that allows the organisation to remain at the competitive edge in its field. For educational organisations this will mean a continual engagement with organisational redesign to ensure that learning is maximised for all learners.

- **Is outward facing, forward looking and distributed**

Ultimately, future leadership will need to monitor the changing external environment continually. It will need to 'look out of the window', and watch for changing trends, or indications that the organisation must rethink its strategy or reposition itself. It will need to ensure that the internal leadership patterns, relationship and connections are best arranged to respond decisively and quickly. In summary, future leadership will be actively, purposively and carefully distributed. In other words, future leadership needs to be orchestrated and distributed in ways that meet the needs of the organisation.

While distributed leadership implies that everyone within the organisation has leadership capability and capacity, in practice leadership will evolve in line with the particular needs of the organisation and its stage of development. It will depend on context, need and situation. Inevitably, distributed leadership will look different in different contexts. It will reflect the inherent diversity and variability of activity within and across networks.

Future leaders will need a repertoire of skills that will allow them to engage with partners. They will need to distribute leadership in a purposeful way that meets the needs of the school and its various partners. They will need to develop new strategies for seeking out, engaging and retaining new partners.

The idea of what constitutes a school is shifting dramatically and irrecoverably. As schools move towards greater partnership working with other schools, external agencies and other organisations, there will be inevitable challenges and periods of rapid change. The wider involvement of service users (parents and students) in decision-making will require careful negotiation about roles and responsibilities. The changes cannot be incremental or ad hoc. Instead they will require considerable re-engineering, and the transformation of professional boundaries and practices.

To be successful, school leaders of the future will have to take the long view of change and development. The challenge for school leaders will be how to keep the long view of change without sacrificing the immediate, and how to build capacity without losing coherence. School leaders will be working in a climate of uncertainty and turbulent change across the system in the next few years. This will mean some abandonment and relinquishment as well as new ways of working.

The transformation of education cannot happen in isolation from the wider societal changes and the reform of the public sector. The structural and cultural changes that are currently underway are substantial, relentless and ultimately non-negotiable. It is inevitable that with such a major transformation, barriers and blockers exist, and will stand in the way of progress. This will require more planned distribution of leadership that matches the need of the school, whatever its form, and its context.

Taking a distributed perspective on leadership means that it is grounded in relational activity (i.e. mutual enquiry, dialogue, partnership) rather than in position or role. Where 'leadership and organisational growth collide it is, by definition, dispersed or distributed' (Hopkins and Jackson, 2003: 13). In very practical terms, it will require the creation of the internal conditions where it can thrive. It will necessitate the creation of time, space and opportunity for groups to meet, plan and reflect. Engaging the many rather than the few in leadership activity is at the heart of distributed leadership. Consider the following questions:

- What needs to happen for leadership to be a more collective, shared and distributed activity within your organisation?
- What challenges might distributed leadership pose and how might these be overcome?
- Where is the leadership potential within your organisation? What would release it?

Final word

The hope of transforming schools through the actions of individual leaders is quickly fading. Strong leaders with exceptional vision and action do exist, but unfortunately they do not come in sufficient quantities to meet the demands and challenges of today's schools. An alternative conceptualisation is one where leadership is understood in terms of shared activities and multiple levels of responsibility.

Early evidence from a research study focusing on highly performing organisations in four sectors – health, education, business and education – indicates that leadership is central to the process of transformation. It shows that organisations performing beyond expectations put their best leaders into positions of significant responsibility, irrespective of their age or stage of career. They also create the organisational infrastructure where their leadership has the maximum benefit within the organisation. They deliberately create the organisational 'spaces' and opportunities for leadership to flourish.

There is some empirical support to suggest a positive relationship between distributed leadership and organisational change. However, as Timperley (2005:417) points out, 'increasing the distribution of leadership is only desirable if the quality of the leadership activities contributes to assisting teachers to provide more effective instruction to their students'. This returns us to the moral purpose of education. We need to be sure that whatever form or forms of leadership we advocate or endorse, it is primarily because there is a positive influence on learning.

Some have warned (Fitzgerald and Gunter, 2007), that distributed leadership could very easily be used to achieve the ends of new public management, in an era where standardisation is not fulfilling its delivery promise. It could be just another way of getting teachers to do more within the palatable discourse of collaboration. It could be a means of fulfilling the demands of an accountability agenda within a framing of apparent democratisation rather than direct imposition.

The evidence, to date, would suggest that these dangers are not materialising, as leadership is being distributed within and between schools not as another means of meeting targets, but as a way of improving learning. However, the potential for distributed leadership to be misused should not be underestimated or ignored.

Schools will need to work together to ensure that their energies in networks, federations and other forms of partnership push the boundaries of challenge, innovation and change. Distributed leadership should not simply be a way of reaching the targets or meeting the next set of demands set by government. The transformational agenda has to be owned by schools and led by schools.

Within this transformational agenda, distributed leadership is neither a good thing nor a bad thing. It will depend. It will depend on the context within which leadership is distributed and the prime aim of the distribution. Flattening the hierarchy or delegating tasks does not necessarily equate with distributed leadership or indeed, result in it. Demolishing structures does not automatically or inevitably improve organisational performance. The nature and quality of leadership *practice* and how it impacts upon *learning* is what matters most.

System transformation will not be achieved by leaders or schools acting alone. Much will depend upon the formation of new networks, partnerships, alliances or federations to share leadership knowledge, address problems and share expertise. System transformation will depend on the way leadership is distributed and cocoordinated within, between and outside schools.

So where does this take us? For some, it takes distributed leadership into the realm of the abstract and away from the practical realities of schooling. For others, it offers the real possibility of looking at leadership through an alternative lens that challenges a taken-for-granted understanding of the relationship between leaders and followers. It suggests that followers may actually be a key element in defining leadership practice through their interactions.

We undoubtedly need new ways of understanding, analysing and making sense of educational transformation in a global world. We need to seek alternative forms of leadership activity that will close the achievement gap. If we are serious about addressing the inequalities in society that are reciprocally and mutually fuelled by the inequalities in education, we must pay greater attention to improving the learning opportunities for all. This means taking a long hard look at our schools and the way they are led.

Distributed leadership certainly isn't a panacea or blueprint for system transformation or organisational improvement. Those who write about it are clear that it doesn't claim to be. But unlike many other theories and labels for leadership, distributed leadership accurately captures the nature of the changes in leadership practice taking place in many organisations, not just schools. In short, whether we like it or not, schools are actively redesigning, realigning and reshaping leadership practice.

As distributed leadership practice develops within and between schools, we certainly need to refine the theory. We also need to know more about the practice as different forms of distributed leadership emerge. We will undoubtedly need to know more about the impact and effects of different forms of distributed leadership practice on organisational learning. Ultimately, if the goal is to build leadership capacity within and across educational systems, we need to implement leadership practices that have a maximum impact upon learning.

Hargreaves (2007) suggests that we urgently need to redefine what public education is for, in a post-standardisation era. He argues that reshaping public education has to be a priority, if we are serious about school and system transformation. As educators, we currently have the opportunity to move the agenda away from a preoccupation with targets to refocus on learning. Such a shift will not be easy; it will necessitate both challenge and risk. But if we consider the alternative, it is a risk well worth taking. It is time to jump the curve.

> *So hope for a great sea change, it means once in a lifetime that justice can rise up and hope and history rhyme*
>
> (Seamus Heaney).

References

Abrahamson, E. (2004). *Change Without Pain*. Cambridge, MA: Harvard Business School Press.

Barber, M. (2007). *Instruction to Deliver*. London: Methuen Press.

Barnard, C. (1968). *Functions of the Executive*. Cambridge, MA: Harvard University Press.

Barr, R.D. and Parrett, W.H. (2007). *The Kids Left Behind: Catching Up the Underachieving Children of Poverty*. Bloomington: Solution Tree.

Barry, D. (1991). 'Managing the bossless team: lessons in distributed leadership'. *Organisational Dynamics*. 21: 31–47.

Beare, H. (2006). *How We Envisage Schooling in the 21st Century*. London: London Specialist Schools and Academies Trust.

Bell, M., Jopling, M., Cordingly, P., Firth, A., King, E. and Mitchell, H. (2006). *What is the impact on pupils of networks that have at least three schools?* Nottingham, UK: NCSL: http://www.ncsl.org.uk/media/02C/23/NLG_rapid_review_full_report.pdf.

Bennet, N., Wise, C., Woods, P. and Harvey, J. (2003). *Distributed Leadership*. Nottingham, NCSL.

Bentley, T. and Gillinson, S. (2007). 'A "D and R System" for education'. London: Innovation Unit.

Berkun, S. (2007). *The Myths of Innovation*. Cambridge, MA: O'Reilly.

Berliner, D. (2005). 'Our impoverished view of Educational Reform'. *Teachers' College Record*. 12(6): 448–452.

Bernake, B. (2006). *Global Economic Integration: What's New and What's Not?* Paper presented at the Federal Reserve bank of Kansas City's 30th Annual Economic Symposium, 25 August: www.federalreserve.gov/boarddocs/speeches/2006.

Bevan, J. (2007). *The Rise and Fall of Marks & Spencer and How it Rose Again*. London: Profile Books.

Bryk, A. and Schneider, B. (2002). *Trust in schools*. USA: Russell Sage Foundation.

Caldwell, B. (2006). *Re-imagining Educational Leadership*. London: ACER Press and Sage.

Camburn, E., Rowan, B. and Taylor, J.E. (2003). 'Distributed leadership in schools: The case of elementary schools adopting comprehensive school reform models' [Electronic version]. *Educational Evaluation and Policy Analysis*. 25(4): 347–373.

Capra, F. (1996). *The Web of Life*. Canada: First Anchor Books.

Capra, F. (2002). *The Hidden Connections*. London: Doubleday.

Castells, M. (1996). *The Information Age: The Rise of the Networked Society*. London: Blackwell.

Chesbrough, H. (2003). 'The Era of Open Innovation'. *MIT Sloan Management Review*. 44(3).

Choo, C. (1998). *The Knowing Organization: How organisations use information to construct meaning, create knowledge, and make decisions*. New York: Oxford University Press.

Collarbone, P. (2005). 'Touching tomorrow: remodelling in English schools'. *Australian Economic Review*, 38(1): 75–82.

Collins, J. (2001). *Good To Great*. New York: Harper Business.

Colwell, H. and Hammersley-Fletcher, L. (2004). 'The emotionally literate primary school'. Paper presented at the *British Educational Research Association Annual Conference*, Manchester.

Copland, M.A. (2003). 'Leadership of inquiry: Building and sustaining capacity for school improvement'. *Educational Evaluation and Policy Analysis*. 24(4): 375–475.

Court, M. (2003). 'Towards democratic leadership: Co-principal initiatives' [Electronic version]. *International Journal of Leadership in Education*. 6(2): 161–183.

Creemers, B. (1994). *The Effective Classroom*. London: Cassell.

Crowther, F., Kaagan, S.S., Ferguson, M. and Hann, L. (2002). *Developing Teacher Leaders: How Teacher Leadership Enhances School Success*. Thousand Oaks, CA: Corwin Press.

Darwin, C, R. (1909). *The Origin of Species*. Harvard Classics. New York: P.F. Collier.

Datnow, A., Hubbard, L., Mehan, H. (2002). *Extending Educational Reform from One School to Many*. London: Falmer Press.

Day, C., Harris, A. and Hadfield, M. (1999). Challenging the Orthodoxy of Effective School Leadership. *American Educational Research Association Conference*, Montreal, Canada.

Day, C., Sammons, P., Harris, A., Hopkins, D., Leithwood, K., Gu, Q., Penlington, C., Mehta, P. and Kington, A. (2007). *The Impact Of School Leadership On Pupil Outcomes*. Interim report to the Department for Children, Schools and Families, London.

DfES (2002). *Time for Standards: Reforming the School Workforce*. DfES/0751/2002, London: HMSO.

DfES (2003). *Raising Standards and Tackling Workload: a National Agreement*. London: HMSO.

DfES (2004). *Every Child Matters*. DfES 1110–2004, London: HMSO.

DfES (2005). *Extended Schools: Access to opportunities and services for all: a prospectus* (184478 451 7). London: HMSO.

DfES (2007). *Independent Study into School Leadership*. London: Price Waterhouse Coopers.

Drath, W.H. and Palus, C.J. (1994). *Making Common Sense: Leadership as meaning-making in a community of practice*. Greensboro, NC: Center for Creative Leadership.

Einstein, A. (1954). *Ideas and Opinions*. New York: Random House.

Elmore, R. (2004). 'Knowing the Right Thing To Do: School Improvement and Performance-Based Accountability'. *NGA Centre for Best Practices*, USA.

Elmore, R. (2006). *The Problem of Capacity in the (Re) Design of Educational Accountability Systems*. Paper presented at 'Examining America's commitment to Closing Achievement Gaps' conference, Teachers College, Columbia University, 13–14 November.

Evans, L. (1998). *Teacher Morale, Job Satisfaction and Motivation*. London: Paul Chapman.

Fink, D. (2006). *Leadership for Mortals: Developing and Sustaining Leaders of Learning*. London: Paul Chapman Press.

Fitzgerald, T. and Gunter, H. (2007). 'Teacher leadership: a new myth for our time'. *American Educational Research Association Conference*, Chicago, USA.

Fletcher, J.K. and Kaufer, K. (2003). 'Shared leadership: Paradox and possibility'. In C.J. Pearce and C. Conger (eds), *Shared Leadership: Reframing the How and Whys of Leadership*. Thousand Oaks, CA: Sage, pp 21–47.

Friedman, T. (2006). *The World is Flat: A Brief History of the Twenty-First Century*. New York: Farrar, Straus and Groux.

Fullan, M. (2001). *Leading in a Culture of Change*. San Francisco, CA: Jossey-Bass.

Fullan, M. (2004). *System thinkers in action: moving beyond the standards plateau*. Nottingham, DfES.

Fullan, M. (2006). *Turnaround Leadership*. San Francisco, CA: Jossey-Bass.

Fullan, M., Hill, P. and Crevola, C. (2007). *Breakthrough*. Thousand Oaks, CA: Corwin Press.

Gastil, J. (1997). *A Definition and Illustration of Democratic Leadership*. Oxford, UK: Oxford University Press (pp. 155–178).

Gibb, C.A. (1954). *Handbook of Social Psychology*. Vol 4, 2nd edn. Reading, MA: Addison-Wesley: pp 205–282.

Giuliani, R. W. (2002). *Leadership*. Miramax Books.

Gladwell, M. (2000). *The Tipping Point*. New York, Little Brown.

Gold, A., Evans, J., Early, P., Halpin, D. and Collabone, P. (2002). *Principled principals? Evidence from ten case studies of 'outstanding' school teachers.* Paper presented at the annual meeting of the American Educational Research Association, New Orleans, LA.

Goldstein, J. (2004). 'Making sense of distributed leadership: the case of peer assistance and review'. *Educational Evaluation and Policy Analysis.* 26(2), 173–197.

Graetz, F. (2000). Strategic change leadership. *Management Decisions.* 38(8): 550–562.

Gronn, P. (2000). 'Distributed properties: A new architecture for leadership'. *Educational Management and Administration.* 28(3): 317–338.

Gronn, P. (2003). *The New Work of Educational Leaders: changing leadership practice in an era of school reform.* London: Paul Chapman.

Gunter, H. and Ribbins, P. (2003). 'Challenging the orthodoxy in school leadership studies: knowers, knowing and knowledge'. *School Leadership and Management.* 23(3): 267–290.

Gurr, D., Drysdale, L. and Mulford, B. (2005). 'Successful principal leadership: Australian case studies'. *Journal of Educational Administration.* 43(6): 539–551.

Hallinger, P. and Heck, R. (1996). 'Reassessing the principal's role in school effectiveness: A review of empirical research 1980–1995'. *Educational Administration Quarterly.* 32(1): 5–44.

Hallinger, P. and Heck, R. (2000). 'Educational change: Opening a window onto leadership as a cultural process'. *School Leadership and Management.* 20(2): 189–205.

Hankin, H. (2005). *The New Workforce: Five Sweeping Trends that will shape your company's future.* New York: Amacom Books.

Hargreaves, A. (2007). *Sustaining Leadership.* Keynote Address, Specialist Schools and Academies Trust National Conference, Birmingham, 28–30 November 2007.

Hargreaves, A. and Fink, D. (2006). *Sustainable Leadership.* San Francisco: Jossey-Bass.

Hargreaves, A. and Shirley, D. (2007). *Raising Achievement: Transforming Learning.* Boston: Lynch School of Education.

Hargreaves, D.H. (2003). *Annual Lecture of the London Leadership Centre.* London Leadership Centre.

Hargreaves, D.H. (2006). *A New Shape for Schooling?* London: Specialist Schools and Academies Trust.

Hargreaves, D.H. (2007). *System Redesign – 1.* London: London Specialist Schools and Academies Trust.

Hargreaves, A., Halasz, G. and Pont, B. (2007). *School Leadership for systemic improvement in Finland.* Paris: OECD.

Harris, A. (2002). 'Effective leadership in schools facing challenging circumstances'. *School Leadership and Management.* 22(1): 15–27.

Harris, A. (2003). 'Teacher leadership, heresy, fantasy or possibility?' *School Leadership and Management*. 23(3): 313–324. ISSN 1363–2434.

Harris, A. (2005). *Crossing Boundaries and Breaking Barriers: Distributing leadership in schools*. Specialist Schools Trust. http://www.sst-inet.net.

Harris, A. (2006). Opening up the Black Box of Leadership Practice: Taking a Distributed Perspective. *International Journal of Educational Administration* 34(2): 37–46.

Harris, A. (2007a). *Deep Leadership and Knowledge Creation*. Interim research report SSAT and NCSL, England.

Harris, A. (2007b). 'Distributed leadership: conceptual confusion and empirical reticence'. *International Journal of Leadership in Education*. 10(3): 1–11.

Harris, A. (2008). *Deep Leadership: An Evaluation*. England: SSAT and NCSL.

Harris, A. and Lambert, L. (2003). *Building Leadership Capacity for School Improvement*. Milton Keynes: Open University Press.

Harris, A. and Muijs, D. (2004). *Improving Schools Through Teacher Leadership*. London: Open University Press.

Harris, A. and Ranson, S. (2005) The contradictions of education policy: disadvantage and achievement *British Educational Research Journal*. 31(5): 571–587.

Harris, A. and Townsend, A. (2007). 'Developing leaders for tomorrow: releasing system potential'. In *School Leadership and Management*. 27(2): pp 169–179, ISSN 1363–2434.

Harris, A., Clarke, P., James, S., Harris, B. and Gunraj, J. (2006b). *Improving Schools in Difficulty*. London: Continuum Press.

Harris, A., Leithwood, K., Day, C., Sammons, P. and Hopkins, D. (2007). 'Distributed leadership and organisational change: reviewing the evidence'. *Journal of Educational Change*. Vol 8 pp 337–347.

Harris, A., Muijs, D. et al (2006a). 'Improving Schools in Challenging Contexts: Exploring the possible School Effectiveness and School Improvement'. *School Effectiveness and School Improvement*. 17(4): 409–425.

Heckscher, C. (2007). *The Collaborative Enterprise*. London: Yale.

Heller, M.F. and Firestone, W. (1995). 'Who's in charge here? Sources of leadership for change in eight schools'. *Elementary School Journal*, 96(1): 65–85.

Hopkins, D. (2001). *School improvement for Real*. London: Falmer Press.

Hopkins, D. and Jackson, D. (2003). 'Building the capacity for leading and learning' in Harris, A., Day, C., Hadfield, M., Hopkins, D., Hargreaves, A. and Chapman, C. *Effective Leadership for School Improvement*. London: Routledge.

Hopkins, D., Harris, A. and Jackson, D. (1997). 'Understanding the school's capacity for development: Growth states and strategies'. *School Leadership and Management*. 17(3): 401–411.

Hutchins, E.T. (1995). *Cognition in the Wild*. Cambridge, MA: MIT.

Imparato, N. and Harari, O. (2007). *Jumping the Curve: Innovation and Strategic Choice in an Age of Transition*. San Francisco: Jossey Bass Business and Management Series.

Jablin, F.M. (1987). 'Formal organisation structure'. In Jablin, F.M., Putnam, L.L., Roberts, K.H. and Porter, L.W. (eds), *Handbook of Organisational Communication: An Interdisciplinary Perspective*. Newbury Park, CA: Sage, pp 389–419.

Jackson, D. and Temperley, J. (2007). 'From professional learning community to networked learning community'. In Stoll, L. and Seashore Louis, K. *Professional Learning Communities*. New York: Open University Press.

Jermier, J.M. and Kerr, S. (1997). 'Substitutes for leadership: Their meaning and measurement – contextual recollections and current observations'. *The Leadership Quarterly*. (8): 95–101.

Keynes, J.M. (1936). *The General Theory of Employment, Interest and Money*. London: Macmillian.

Klein, N. (2007). *The Shock Doctrine: The Rise of Disaster Capitalism*. New York: Metropolitan Books.

Krogh, G., Ichijo, K. and Nonaka, I. (2006). *Enabling Knowledge Creation*. Oxford: Oxford University Press.

Kuhn, T.S. (1962). *The Structure of Scientific Revolutions*. Chicago: University of Chicago Press.

Lakomski, G. (2005). *Managing Without Leadership: Towards a Theory of Organisational Functioning*. London: Elsevier.

Lashway, L. (2003). 'Distributed Leadership'. *Research Roundup*. 19(4): 1–6.

Lave, J. and Wenger, E. (1991) *Situated Learning: Legitimate Peripheral Participation*. Cambridge, MA: Cambridge University Press.

Leithwood, K. and Jantzi, D. (2000). The effects of different sources of leadership on student engagement in school. In Riley, K. and Louis, K. (eds), *Leadership For Change and School Reform*. London: Routledge, pp 50–66.

Leithwood, K., Seashore-Louis, K., Anderson, S. and Wahlstrom, K. (2004). *How Leadership Influences Student Learning: A review of research for the Learning from Leadership Project*, New York: Wallace Foundation.

Leithwood, K., Mascall, B., Strauss, T., Sacks, R., Memon, N. and Yashkina, A. (2006a). 'Distributing leadership to make schools smarter'. *Leadership and Policy*. 6(1): 37–67.

Leithwood, K., Day, C., Sammons, P., Harris, A. and Hopkins, D. (2006b), *Seven Strong Claims about Successful Leadership*. London: DfES.

Leithwood, K., Day, C., Sammons, P., Harris, A. and Hopkins, D. (2007). *Leadership and Student Learning Outcomes, Interim Report*. London: DCSF.

Leithwood et al (2008). *Distributed Leadership*. Netherlands: Springer Press.

Levin, M. (2006). 'Can research improve educational leadership?' *Educational Researcher.* 35(8): 38–44.

Levine, A. (2005). *Educating School Leaders.* New York: The Education School Project.

Lieberman, A. (2007). 'Professional learning communities: a reflection'. In Stoll, L. and Seashore-Louis, K., *Professional Learning Communities.* New York: Open University Press.

Lima, A. (2007). Teachers' professional development in departmentalised, loosely coupled organisations: Lessons for school improvement from a case study of two curriculum departments. *School Effectiveness and School Improvement.* 18(3): 273–301.

Little, J.W. (1990). The persistence of privacy: Autonomy and initiative in teachers' professional relations. *Teachers College Record.* 91(4): 509–536.

Lindsay, G., Muijs, D., Harris, A., Chapman, C., Arweck, E. and Goodall, J. (2007). *Evaluation of Federations,* Final Report, London: DCSF.

Locke, E.A. (2002). 'The leaders as integrator: The case of Jack Welch at General Electric'. In Neider, L.L. and Schriesheim, C. (eds), *Leadership.* Greenwich, CT: Information Age Publishing, pp 1–22.

MacBeath, J. (ed.) (1998). *Effective School Leadership: Responding to Change.* London: Paul Chapman.

MacBeath, J. (2005). 'Leadership as distributed: a matter of practice'. *School Leadership & Management.* 25(4): 349–366.

McKinsey & Company (2007). *How the World's Best Performing Systems Come Out On Top.* London: McKinsey.

Mantell, W. (2007). *Education by numbers: the damaging treadmill of school tests.* London: Politico.

Martin, J. and Frost, P. (1996). 'The organisational culture war games: A struggle for intellectual dominance'. In Clegg, S.R., Hardy, C. and Nord, W.R. (eds), *Handbook of Organisational Studies.* London: Sage, pp 599–621.

Marzano, R.J., Waters, T. and McNulty, B.A. (2005). *School Leadership That Works: From Research to Results.* Alexandria, VA: Association for Supervision and Curriculum Development.

Morrisey, M. (2000). *Professional Learning Communities: An Ongoing Exploration.* Austin, TX: Southwest Educational Development Laboratory.

Murphy, J. (1988). 'The characteristics of instructionally effective school districts'. *Journal of Educational Research.* 81(3): 176–181.

Murphy, J. (2005). *Connecting Teacher Leadership and School Improvement.* Thousand Oaks, CA: Corwin Press.

Murphy, J. and C. Meyers (2008). *Turning Around Failing Schools: Leadership Lessons From the Corporate and Non-Profit Sectors.* Thousand Oaks, CA: Corwin Press.

Murphy, J., Goldring, E. and Porter, A. (2006). *Leadership for Learning: A Research-Based Model and Taxonomy of Behaviours.* Wallace Foundation State Action for Educational Leadership Conference. Saint Louis.

NCSL (2006). *Succession Planning: Formal Advice to the Secretary of State.* Nottingham: NCSL.

Nias, J., Southworth, Geoff; Yeomans, Robin (1989). 'The culture of collaboration. Chapter 4 in *Staff Relationships in the Primary School.* London: Cassell, pp 47–74.

Nonaka, I. and Takeuchi, H. (1995). *The Knowledge-Creating Company: How Japanese Companies Create the Dynamics of Innovation.* Oxford: Oxford University Press.

Obolensky, N. (2008). 'Chaos Leadership and Polyarchy – countering leadership stress?' *Extended Essay Series, Centre for Leadership Studies,* University of Exeter.

Ogawa, R.T. and Bossert, S.T. (1995). 'Leadership as an Organisational Quality'. *Educational Administration Quarterly*: 31.

OECD Centre for Educational Research and Innovation (CERI) (2000). *Innovating Schools.* Paris: OECD.

OECD (CERI) (2005). Istance, D., Ackalen, P. and Vincent Lancrin, S. *Schooling for Tomorrow.* Paris: OECD September.

OfSTED (2000). 'Educational inequality, mapping race, class . . .'. London: Office for Standards in Education.

OfSTED (2007). *Reforming and Developing the School Workforce.* London: HMSO.

Pearce, C.J. and Conger, C. (2003). *Shared Leadership: Reframing the Hows and Whys of Leadership.* Thousand Oaks, CA: Sage.

Peterson, K.D. (2002). 'The professional development of principals: innovations and opportunities', in Young, M.D. *Ensuring the University's Capacity to Prepare Learning Focused Leadership.* Columbia, MO: National Commission for the Advancement of Educational Leadership Preparation.

Portin, B.S. (1998). 'Compounding roles: A study of Washington's principals'. *International Journal of Educational Research.* 29(4): 381–391.

Pounder, D.G., Ogawa, R.T. and Adams, E.A. (1995). 'Leadership as an organisationwide phenomena: Its impact on school performance'. *Educational Administration Quarterly.* 31(4): 564–588.

Prigogine, I. (1985). *Order out of Chaos.* New York, Bantam.

Reich, R. (2000). *The Future of Success: Working and Living in the New Economy.* New York: First Vintage Books.

Resnick, L.B. and Spillane, J.P. (2006). From individual learning to organisational designs for learning', in Verschaffel, L., Dochy, F., Boekaerts, M. and Vosniadou, S. (eds), *Instructional Psychology: Past, Present and Future Trends. Sixteen essays in honor of Erik De Corte* (Advances in Learning and Instruction Series). Oxford: Pergamon.

Reynolds, D., Harris, A., Clarke, P., Harris, B. and James, S. (2006). 'Challenging the Challenged: Improving Schools in exceptionally challenging circumstances'. *School Effectiveness and School Improvement.* 17(4): 425–441, ISSN 0924–3453.

Reynolds, D., Sammons, P., Stoll, L. and Barber, M. (1995). 'School Effectiveness and School Improvement in the United Kingdom'. Chapter 5 in Cheemers, B.P.M. and Osinga, N. (eds), *ICSEI Country Report*. Leeuwarden, The Netherlands: ICSEI, 21: 60–80.

Rosenholtz, S.J. (1989). *Teachers' Workplace: The Social Organization of Schools*. New York: Longman.

Schumpeter, J.A. (1942). *The Process of Creative Destruction*. London, Unwin.

Senge, P. (1990). *The Fifth Discipline. The art and practice of the learning organisation*. New York: Doubleday.

Senge, P. et al (1994). *The Fifth Discipline Fieldbook: Strategies and Tools for Building a Learning Organization*. New York: Doubleday.

Senge, P., Kleiner, A., Roberts, C., Ross, R., Roth, G. and Smith, B. (1999). *The Dance of Change: The Challenges of Sustaining Momentum in Learning Organizations*. New York: Doubleday/Currency).

Senge, P., Scharmer, C.O., Jawroski, J. and Flowers, B. (2005). *Presence – Exploring Profound Change in People, Organisations and Society*. London: Nicholas Brealey Publishing.

Sergiovanni, T.J. (1992). 'Leadership as stewardship: "Who's serving who?" ' *Moral Leadership: Getting to the Heart of School Improvement*. San Francisco, Jossey-Bass: 119–140.

Sergiovanni, T.J. (2001). 'New Leadership, roles and competencies'. In *Leadership: What's in it for Schools?* London, Routledge Falmer: 38–58.

Shelley, H. (1960). 'Focused leadership and cohesiveness in small groups'. *Sociometry*. 23: 209–216.

Silins, H. and Mulford, W. (2002). *Leadership and School Results*. Dordrecht, The Netherlands: Kluwer.

Smylie, M. and Hart, A. (1999). 'School leadership for teacher learning and change: A human and social capital development perspective'. In J. Murphy and K.S. Louis (eds), *Handbook of research on educational administration* (2nd edn). San Francisco: Jossey-Bass: 421–441.

Spillane, J.P. (2006). *Distributed Leadership*. San Francisco, CA: Jossey-Bass.

Spillane, J.P. and Camburn, E. (2006). The practice of leading and managing: The distribution of responsibility for leadership and management in the schoolhouse. *American Educational Research Association*. San Francisco, CA.

Spillane, J. and Diamond, J.B. (2007) *Distributed Leadership in Practice*. New York: Teachers College Press, Columbia University.

Spillane, J.P., Zoltners Sherer, J. (2004). 'A Distributed Perspective on School Leadership: Leadership Practice as Stretched Over People and Place'. Paper prepared for presentation at the *Annual Meeting of the American Educational Research Association*, San Diego, April.

Spillane, J.P., Diamond, J.B. and Jita, L. (2003). 'Leading instruction: The distribution of leadership for instruction' [Electronic version]. *Journal of Curriculum Studies*. 35(5): 533–543.

Spillane, J.P., Halverson, R. and Diamond, J.B. (2001). 'Towards a theory of leadership practice: A distributed perspective'. *Journal of Curriculum Studies.* 36(1): 3–34.

Spillane, J.P., Camburn, E. and Pareja, A.S. (2007). Taking a distributed perspective to the school principal's workday. *Leadership and Policy in Schools.* 6(1): 103–125.

Stiglitz, J. (2006). 'Make globalisation work for everyone'. *The Straights Times.* 8 September, 25.

Stoll, L. and Fink, D. (1996). *Changing Our Schools.* Buckingham: Open University Press. 13: 1–12.

Stoll, L. and Seashore-Louis, K. (2007). *Professional Learning Communities.* New York: Open University Press.

Storey, A. (2004). 'The problem of distributed leadership in schools'. *School Leadership & Management.* 24(3): 249–265.

Sullivan, H. and Skelcher, C. (2003). 'Working Across Boundaries: Collaboration in Public Services', *Health & Social Care in the Community.* 11(2): 185.

Surowiecki, James (2004). *The Wisdom of Crowds: Why the Many Are Smarter Than the Few and How Collective Wisdom Shapes Business, Economies, Societies and Nations.* New York: Little, Brown.

Taylor, C. (2004). *Modern Social Imaginaries.* New York: Duke University Press.

Timperley, H. (2005). 'Distributed Leadership: Developing theory from practice'. *Journal of Curriculum Studies.* 37(4): 395–420.

Toffler, A. (1985). *The Adaptive Corporation.* London: Pan Books.

Townsend, T. (ed.) (2007). *International Handbook of School Effectiveness and School Improvement.* Netherlands: Springer.

Vroom, V. and Yago, A.I. (1998). *Situation Effects and Levels of Analysis in the Study of Leadership Participation.* Stamford, CT: JAI Press.

Wageman, R., Nunes, D., Burruss, J. and Hackman, J. (2008). *Senior Leadership Teams: What it takes to make them great.* Cambridge:Harvard Business School Press.

Ward, Helen and Bloom, Adi (2007). 'Test drive harms links with parents'. *Times Educational Supplement.* 14 December.

Weick, K.E. (1976). 'Educational organisations as loosely coupled systems'. *Phi Delta Kappan.* 63(10): 673–676.

Wenger, E. (1998). *Communities of Practice: Learning Meaning and Identity.* New York: Cambridge University Press.

Wenger, E., McDermott, R. and Snyder, W. (2000). *Cultivating Communities of Practice: A Guide to Managing Knowledge.* Cambridge, MA Harvard Business School Press.

Wheatley, M. (1999). *Leadership and the New Science.* San Francisco: Berrett Koehler.

West, A. and Penell, H. (2003). *Underachievement in Schools.* London: Routledge.

Wilkinson, R.G. (2005). *The Impact of Inequality: How to Make Sick Societies Healthier*. New York: New Press.

Youngs, H. (2007). 'Having the presence and courage to see beyond the familiar: Challenging our habitual assumptions of school leadership'. *Paper presented at ACEL and ASCD Conference*, 10–12 October, Sydney.

Zhao, Y. (2007). 'Education in the Flat World'. *Phi Delta Kappa International*. 2(4): 3–18.

Zuboff, S. and Maxim, J. (2002). *The Support Economy*. London: Penguin.

Index

Please note that references to Notes will have the letter 'n' following the note. Page references to any Figures or Tables will be in *italic* print